If You
Build It,
They Will
Learn

If You Build It, They Will Learn

17 Devices for Demonstrating Physical Science

by Bruce Yeany

NSTApress
NATIONAL SCIENCE TEACHERS ASSOCIATION
Arlington, Virginia

NATIONAL SCIENCE TEACHERS ASSOCIATION

Claire Reinburg, Director
Judy Cusick, Senior Editor
Andrew Cocke, Associate Editor
Betty Smith, Associate Editor
Robin Allan, Book Acquisitions Coordinator

ART AND DESIGN
Will Thomas, Director
Linda Olliver, cover art
Bruce Yeany, photographs and interior illustration

PRINTING AND PRODUCTION
Catherine Lorrain-Hale, Director
Nguyet Tran, Assistant Production Manager
Jack Parker, Electronic Prepress Technician

NATIONAL SCIENCE TEACHERS ASSOCIATION
Gerald F. Wheeler, Executive Director
David Beacom, Publisher

Library of Congress Cataloging-in-Publication Data

Yeany, Bruce.
 If you build it, they will learn : 17 devices for demonstrating physical science / by Bruce Yeany.
    p. cm.
 Includes bibliographical references.
 ISBN-13: 978-0-87355-267-7
 ISBN-10: 0-87355-267-9
 1. Science--Study and teaching (Elementary)--Activity programs. 2. Science--Study and teaching (Middle school)--
Activity programs. I. Title.
 LB1585.Y43 2006
 372.3'5--dc22
                                    2006010887

Table of Contents

Preface vii

Introduction
Why Build It? 1
Building the Device 5
Safety First 6
Common Construction Practices 8

Devices
1 Galileo's Track 11
Instructional Information 11
Directions for Assembly 18

2 Can You Top This? 25
Instructional Information 25
Directions for Assembly—Wood Version 36
Directions for Assembly—Student Model 40

3 Inertia Block 43
Instructional Information 43
Directions for Assembly 49

4 Resonant Pendulums 55
Instructional Information 55
Directions for Assembly—Coupled Pendulum 65
Directions for Assembly—Wilberforce Pendulum Wood Model 69
Directions for Assembly—Wilberforce Pendulum Clay Ball Model 76

5 Hero's Fountainn 81
Instructional Information 81
Directions for Assembly 88

6 String Racers 97
Instructional Information 97
Directions for Assembly—Propellers 102
Directions for Assembly—Balloons 112

7 Solar Motor 115
Instructional Information 115
Directions for Assembly 121

Table of Contents

8 Weigh Your Cans 133
Instructional Information 133
Directions for Assembly 144

9 Balanced Breakfast Box 151
Instructional Information 151
Directions for Assembly 159

10 Heavy Foam 163
Instructional Information 163
Directions for Assembly 172

11 Mystery Boxes 175
Instructional Information 175
Directions for Assembly—Wooden Box 181
Directions for Assembly—Cardboard Box 189

12 Balloon in a Bottle 193
Instructional Information 193
Directions for Assembly 200

13 Hot, Warm, or Cold? 205
Instructional Information 205
Directions for Assembly 212

14 What Color Is Inside? 215
Instructional Information 215
Directions for Assembly—Paint Can 221
Directions for Assembly—Cardboard Box 226

15 Gum Wrapper Thermostat 229
Instructional Information 229
Directions for Assembly 234

16 Simple Motor, Two-Coil Motor 241
Instructional Information 241
Directions for Assembly—Student Motors 247
Directions for Assembly—Two-Coil Motors 251

17 Lightbulbs 257
Instructional Information 257
Directions for Assembly—Filament Board 264
Directions for Assembly—Jelly Jar Lightbulb 269

Appendix A—Resources 277
Appendix B—Research Review 279

Preface

Science supply companies offer more materials than a classroom could possibly use, so why would any teacher want to build his or her own demonstration pieces? For starters, some of you may have problems with equipment cost, quality, size for classroom needs, and availability of a product. Or you may want to be able to adjust variables to meet specific student needs and to gain a sense of accomplishment when you complete the task. You will find using pieces of equipment you have built for yourself extremely satisfying, and you may gain a deeper understanding of the concepts you want to teach. Perhaps most important, building or having students build equipment helps create an environment rich in opportunities for students to make observations and investigate ideas.

When I've demonstrated the devices in this book at workshops and inservice programs, I've found many people who want to make their own equipment but are lacking in two fundamental areas: how to construct and how to use the equipment within the classroom setting. This book addresses those areas.

Step-by-step directions for the device are given in the second part of each section—"Directions for Assembly." Some of you may find the building section more detailed than you need, but I want to be sure anyone can make these devices—even those who are unaccustomed to building these types of projects. If you lack any of the tools or skills needed, look for help from a variety of people—students, friends, parents, or other teachers, possibly those who are in the school shop programs.

Once the equipment is built, you will need to know the best way to use it. Each section starts with suggestions for instruction—"Instructional Information." Good demonstrations and activities need the proper groundwork laid before they are used. You must verify that students are learning the concepts set out as the objective during and after each demonstration is performed in the classroom, and this part will help you do that. You will probably want to add ideas of your own.

Bruce Yeany

Why Build It?

Demonstrations and equipment should continue to play a role in the acquisition of knowledge. Research overwhelmingly supports using materials that can help discover or redefine how the processes of science operate. What is also clear is that teachers must use demonstration and exploratory materials with a clear, well-thought-out purpose in mind. The days of unconnected demonstrations for the fun of it are gone.

You need to establish what knowledge students already possess and then determine what methods will build effectively on the established base. In some cases, you should use inquiry and discovery methods before discussing concepts. Or you could use lecture demonstrations followed by activities that would clarify the conceptual knowledge.

You must make sure that students are not passive learners, whatever your method of instruction. Students must be involved, whether through hands-on activities, diagramming, interactive discussions, Socratic questioning, or other techniques.

Research reaffirms that science can be as interesting as we want it to be. A classroom filled with materials to explore will spark a student's interest in the subject matter. The moment students walk into your room, something should prod them on to further studies. A science room indistinguishable from any other classroom can impart only a neutral or even negative attitude toward the subject matter. This not only makes the teacher's job harder, but also can determine the degree of success students will have within your classroom.

Improving Learning Through Demonstrations

There is strong pedagogical argument to be made in favor of using demonstrations in the classroom. If the demonstration is going to achieve any of the lofty goals that the National Science Education Standards (NRC 1996) have described, however, it must be carried out effectively. Here are a few guidelines that can increase the effectiveness of equipment and teacher demonstrations.

- Present real science, not a sideshow. Demonstrations should serve serious educational purposes. Avoid demonstrations in which the concepts will not be studied.
- Keep demonstrations as simple as possible while still making your point. Complex demonstrations tend to confuse students and may lead to reinforcing misconceptions.
- Use examples that students can relate to. Concepts are easier to understand when students are familiar with the demonstrated materials.
- Encourage students to try experiments for themselves. Give them opportunities for additional research and exploration.
- Have students predict the outcomes of a demonstration by themselves and then have them discuss their predictions with other students before seeing the demonstration.

- Use discrepant events sparingly. Don't leave discrepant events as a misconception; make sure students understand the concept before continuing.
- Have students explain their observations to others.
- Ask questions of students and encourage them to ask questions of you. Ask students to explain what they saw. Have students use diagrams to illustrate the demonstrated concept.
- Have students observe, write, and explain. Students need to show understanding of concepts. Do not assume that they "got it."
- Make the demonstration visible. If students cannot see what happens, there is no reason to demonstrate.
- Do not be afraid of failure. An experiment that does not work can be a learning experience.
- Keep demonstration pieces in plain view. Too many pieces of equipment stay locked up in closets, never to see the light of day, or are shown only for brief periods. Keep your demonstration pieces out for days after a demonstration.

Classroom Guidelines

Each of the devices in this book is in a single section consisting of two parts "Instructional Information," and "Directions for Assembly."

"Instructional Information," the first part of each section, reviews the intended concept and how it can be presented in the classroom setting. "Instructional Information" includes explanations and examples and may list brief instructions for creating additional activities. This part is broken down and labeled with the following subheadings.

Picture and Overview

Each chapter starts with a photo or photos of the completed device. The overview briefly describes the concept demonstrated by each piece and how the device can be used.

Student Skills

Each device and its suggested additional activities offer the students a platform on which to build or "construct" several educational processes and skills. In many cases, the demonstrations are just the starting point for more advanced studies. To expand the demonstrations beyond the point of entertainment, you should identify what skills you want to concentrate on and then develop stronger lessons in those areas. One or more skills or processes related to the activity are listed under this subhead.

Related Concepts or Processes

This list suggests areas of study in which the device can be used. You can use it also as a list of vocabulary terms.

Prior Knowledge

The term *prior knowledge* is essential. Using demonstrations when students don't have a basis of understanding is merely entertainment. This section suggests underlying principles that will help students understand the device. The ideas listed are the concepts you can lay as groundwork for understanding for the ideas to follow. Without prior knowledge, demonstrations can promote or reinforce misconceptions that become harder to correct with the passage of time.

Predemonstration Discussion

This subhead is an extension of the prior knowledge subhead. Although it is difficult to suggest all possible scenarios that lead to the use of each device, this section reviews the most basic concepts. It contains questions that can be used for discussions and, in several cases, suggests activities that can review prior knowledge concepts. You can review quickly or extensively, depending on your classroom requirements. In either case, going over the concepts listed here will be beneficial to students when they view the demonstration.

Suggestions for Presentation

This subhead suggests methods for presenting the device and questions for discussion. The sequences of interactive questions will guide students to an understanding of the concept rather than their being dependent solely on instructor explanations. The questions will promote discussions about the action of each device. You should develop additional questions that apply to your specific objectives. The intent of questions is to have students arrive at their own understanding and then demonstrate understanding by answering questions. You should listen carefully through the questioning process to determine that students have reached the level of knowledge they need. It is better to ask too many questions rather than too few. Many times we as instructors assume that students have grasped the concept only to find out later that they have missed central points of a demonstration.

Postdemonstration Activities

This segment offers additional methods for exploring the central concepts given in the primary demonstration. It may include additional questions for discussion, opportunities for writing prompts, variations of the demonstration, and additional experiments to try.

Discussion of Results

The discussion of results is intended primarily for you. It is a brief explanation of what the device does and how it works. It explains the concept that is demonstrated. You can modify the explanation to the level you want for your students.

Additional Activities

This segment offers additional pieces or activities for further study. Students can explore some of the ideas offered in this section on their own as a science project or as an independent study.

Reference

National Research Council (NRC). 1996. *National Science Education Standards.* Washington, DC: National Academy Press. Online version at *www.nap.edu/books/0309053269/html/index.html.*

Building the Device

"Directions for Assembly," the second part of each section gives a detailed, illustrated procedure on how to build each demonstration piece. In chapters in which directions for more than one piece are given, each is listed separately. This part of each section has two segments.

Materials

Everything needed to build the device is listed here. Common items such as varnish and tape may be omitted.

Directions for Assembly

This section is a step-by-step guide that explains in detail how to build each piece. Pictures and drawings have been included as visual aids. These pieces have been constructed using the minimum number of tools. In many cases, the wood dimensions are matched to existing purchased wood widths. The dimensions in these pieces are not critical and can be changed to fit available supplies. You don't need a complete woodshop to produce the devices. The list of power tools has been kept to a minimum, but they would make the production easier. Please refer to the manufacturer's instructions for proper and safe use of each tool listed.

Suggested Tools

- Drill with a set of drill bits—a counter sink for screws would also be very useful
- Screwdrivers, Phillips and slotted blade
- Saw—many options here include handsaw, circular saw, miter box, saber saw, band saw, and table saw
- Balance or spring scale
- Sander—a powered hand sander or belt sander would be helpful but is not required
- Propane torch or other heat source
- Carpenter's square
- Pencil
- Scissors
- Sandpaper, medium to fine grit
- Paintbrush

Safety First

Safety should be everyone's first concern, whether it's in the classroom with students or in the workshop preparing materials for use in the classroom. Safety notes accompany each piece. Pay attention to them.

Equipment

The safety equipment shown here is inexpensive and may save you from a trip to the doctor.

The type of goggles shown provides protection from flying objects and from irritating dust particles. NSTA recommends that you use safety goggles that conform to the ANSI Z87.1 standard and that provide both impact and chemical-splash protection for all science laboratory work.

The dust mask provides good protection from breathing in dust particles while cutting or sanding; however, it is not adequate for blocking fumes from varnishing.

A long sleeved shirt and leather gloves complete the wardrobe for safety. The leather gloves are particularly useful when you are holding wooden parts during sawing, drilling, and sanding.

Whenever possible, cut, drill, and sand outside. It helps reduce the amount of sawdust that gets spread around inside the house.

Staining and varnishing of the finished pieces should be done outside to help reduce fumes inside the house.

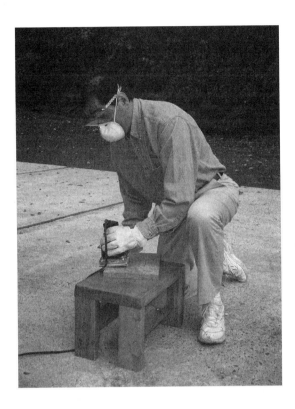

Common Construction Practices

In some of the sections, photographs will show wood parts being held by hand during the cutting and drilling process. This was done only to make the instructions clear. It is not the best or safest method for construction.

Using a clamp or clamps is one alternative to holding parts by hand. Several types of clamps are available and can be found in most hardware stores. The wood is shown clamped down to a workstation. This is more secure and safe than holding it in your hand and will yield greater precision in cuts and drilled holes.

Using a vise is the safest and most secure method for holding pieces of wood during construction.

Clamping wood pieces in the vise can also be helpful when sanding. With the vise holding the wood securely, you smooth the edges with a sander while you use a hose from a vacuum to capture most of the dust particles.

Several of the devices need screws to hold pieces of wood together. A countersink drill bit is a cheap but practical purchase for use during the construction of these pieces.

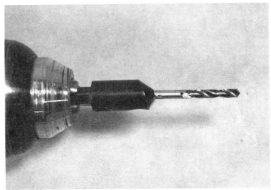

Screws put into an ordinary hole can split the wood due to the large screw-head size. The countersink drill bit will drill a hole for the shaft of the screw. The black portion of the countersink should be drilled into the wood deep enough to fit the head of the screw.

If You Build It, They Will Learn

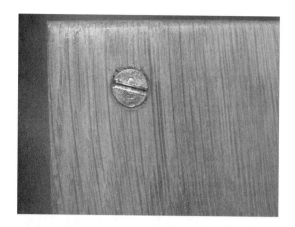

The face of the screw should be slightly beneath the surface of the wood into which it is screwed. This will keep the sharp edge of the screw head from scratching against other surfaces.

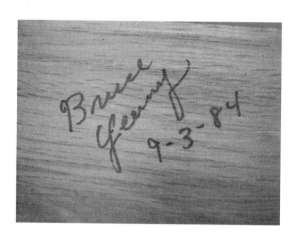

Sign your name! If you make the effort to build a project, take time to sign it and add the date. It adds a nice personal touch and you will appreciate it years later—as you can see from the photograph.

Instructional Information

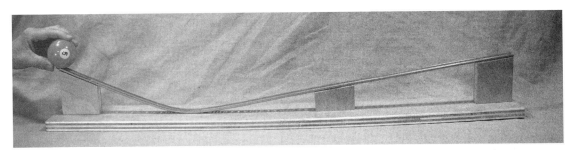

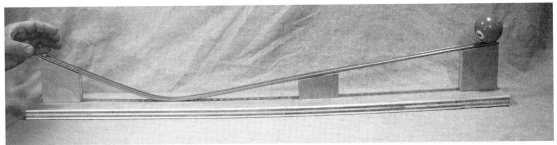

Overview

Galileo's track is made from one long continuous rail that joins two different angled ramps together. The first ramp of the track has a short, steep slope. After a ball or marble rolls down this first ramp, it will then roll up a longer gently sloping part of the track on the opposite ramp. With both sides of the track at the same height, the questions to be asked center around how far a ball will roll up the opposing hill when released from either of the sides. It was with such a track that Galileo studied the motion of objects, and it led him to the concept of inertia.

Student Skills

Prediction. Have students list all of the possible results of rolling the ball down one ramp and then the other ramp. Then have them predict the most likely outcome for each trial.

Application. Have students identify similar situations in which acceleration is determined by the steepness of an incline.

Measurements and Data. Have students run trials to determine if a change in the angles or height of a ramp will change the final velocity of a ball rolling down a track.

Historical Research. Have students research the life and contributions made by Galileo in several areas of science and his methods of investigation.

Conclusion. Students can conclude that height and friction are the two variables that will determine the final velocity of a ball rolling down a track. The angle will determine the rate of acceleration.

Related Concepts or Processes

Speed
Potential energy
Kinetic energy
Inertia
Newton's first law

Acceleration
Mechanical energy
Friction
Rotational inertia
Law of conservation of energy

Prior Knowledge

The Galileo track is very easy to operate, and it is this simplicity that makes it appealing to students of all ages. Elementary school students can play with it as a toy, but introducing some basic science concepts can turn it into a learning tool. Students at this age may have some understanding that gravity is the force pulling the ball down the ramps. They should also know that a ball should speed up—accelerate—as it rolls down a ramp. Intuition will tell them that the balls will accelerate at different rates. At this age they know that objects slow down due to something called friction, but they may not know why.

Middle school students should be able to identify that the ball has potential energy that changes into kinetic energy as it rolls down the track. They should be able to define acceleration as a rate, and they may have been introduced to Galileo's idea of inertia.

Predemonstration Discussion

Before using Galileo's track, a 4- to 6-foot piece of shelving track can be a simple tool to review some concepts about motion. This track, available at any hardware store, is used for holding shelving brackets. The ball can be purchased through a science catalog. Other solid balls are suitable for use, such as a pool ball.

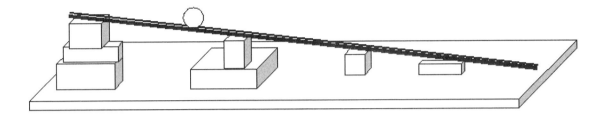

Some questions that can be discussed include the following:
- What happens to the speed of the ball as it rolls down the ramp?
- How would the acceleration change if the ramp were steeper?
- How would starting the ball at a lower position on the track affect its acceleration?
- Where does the ball have the greatest potential energy on this track?
- As the balls roll down the track, what happens to the potential energy?
- What happens to the ball if it rolls up the track?

Roll the ball from the bottom of the track upward so that it has just enough speed to reach the top and then roll back down.
- How does the acceleration going up a ramp compare to acceleration coming down a ramp?

You might want to discuss that Galileo performed similar experiments. He argued that, as the angle of incline of a track is increased, the motion of a rolling ball approaches free fall, so that the motion of the ball down the track is the same type of accelerated motion as an object falling straight down.

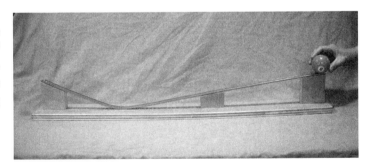

Suggestions for Presentation

Set the device on a table for students to view it before you demonstrate it. Develop a discussion around how a ball will act on the device. Ask students to predict the result before allowing a ball to roll from one ramp to the other. Before demonstrating, point out that both ramps are the same height. A ball sitting on either ramp will have the same amount of potential energy.

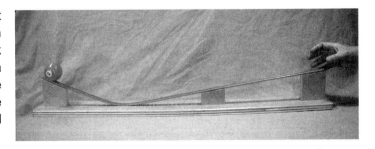

After releasing the ball from one ramp and observing the results, try releasing it from the other. Allow the ball to continue to roll and point out that each successive movement up the opposite ramp is shorter than the previous movement.

Interactive questions to ask during presentation include:
- Which position will allow the ball to reach the bottom the quicker?
- Which side accelerates the ball to a higher speed? How might this be tested?
- Will the ball be able to roll off of one ramp when released from the opposite side?
- After releasing the ball from both sides, note that the ball does not quite reach the same height from which it was released. Why?
- Why does the ball go a slightly shorter distance for each trip on the track?
- What is causing the ball to lose energy?
- The energy lost to friction is changed into what new forms of energy?
- If one side of the track were to be propped up 1 inch higher than the other side, what would happen if the ball were rolled from the higher side?
- Instead of propping up one side, suggest that the longer side was doubled and then tripled in length but remained at the same height.
  - What would happen to the angle?
  - What would be the effect?
  - What would be the result if the longer side were laid flat?

If you are using this demonstration at the beginning of the study of the concept of inertia, refer to Galileo's argument about making the second slope longer and longer until it becomes horizontal. The ball should continue at the same speed "forever."

Postdemonstration Activities and Discussion

Have students research and apply the lessons to existing situations. For example, a roller coaster's track changes a car's potential energy into kinetic energy. Why must each successive hill on the track be smaller than the previous one?

Research Galileo and his rationale for the concept of inertia. How did his views on motion differ from those of Aristotle?

For another study, you can set up two inclined planes on a table. Two pieces of shelving brackets are needed. One piece should be twice as long as the other. A single metal or glass ball can be used and alternated from one track to the other, or two identical balls can be used simultaneously. The balls should be ¾-inch diameter or larger to fit properly on the track. Prop both pieces up to the same height. You might need to screw the tracks into the blocks that are supporting them. Or, you can make permanent frames similar in construction to the original ramp design. The ends of the track must be bent so that the balls will travel horizontally as they leave the track.

Position the ends of the track at the edge of the table. Have students write possible outcomes if the balls are released and allowed to land on the floor. Which track will give a ball the greater final velocity? The answer is that each ball should land the same distance away from the table when it leaves each track.

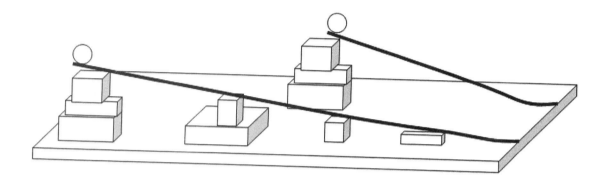

Discussion of Results

The framing of the Galileo track should position the top of both tracks at the same height from their bases. If balls are lifted to the top of either track, they are given the same amount of energy because the elevation of each track is the same. This is referred to as giving the ball potential energy. Release the ball from one ramp and then the other, and note that the balls accelerate at different rates down the ramps. When students watch the ball roll down the longer ramp, the acceleration is slow enough that they can observe that the speed is increasing as the ball travels down the track. On the short steep ramp, it is much harder to observe the acceleration because it is a higher rate for a shorter period of time.

If you set up the suggested postdemonstration, release the ball from the same height on each track; the final velocity coming off of each track will be the same. The ball will fall the same distance when it leaves the end of each track. The amount of time each ball is falling down each track is the same, so if the balls land the same distance away from the table, they should have exited the track with the same velocity.

As the ball rolls down the track, the potential energy (in this case energy stored due to an upward change in position against gravity) changes into kinetic energy. During the downward movement, the ball is rolling and the rate of rotation increases as it continues to roll. This energy gained by rolling is called rotational kinetic energy. Since the ball is moving, it has a second type of energy called translational kinetic energy; this is energy that is due to movement from one location to another. This translational kinetic energy also increases as the speed increases.

By the time the ball reaches the bottom of the track, all of the potential energy is converted into the kinetic energies. Both forms of kinetic energy convert back into potential energy as the ball rolls up the other side of the ramp. The ball will momentarily stop on the other side at a position very close to the original starting height from the first side. The ball cannot quite reach the same height because it loses small amounts of kinetic energy as it moves. Some of the energy goes into the track itself. This can be felt by touching the base when the ball is in motion. Clamping the track base to the tabletop can reduce the wasted energy going into the track.

The ball also has rotational friction. This is caused by the interference of small indentations or deformities as one surface rolls over another. In a rolling motion, friction causes the ball to rotate and stops any sliding and slipping motion.

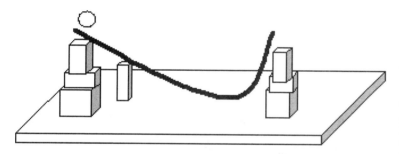

If the track is made too steep on the shorter side, the ball will not reach nearly the same height as the release point. On a very steep track, the ball will slip as it tries to roll upward. If the ball slips it can't move forward or, in this case, upward. If the ball slips, then the height reached is due primarily to the translational kinetic energy. This rolling friction and slipping can be easily shown with an additional piece of the shelf tracking. This track can be bent to have one side with a very steep angle and can be propped up temporarily by some stacks of blocks. Tape or screw the track to the blocks to make it more stable. Note that when the ball is rolled down from the left side of the track, it is not able to climb up very far on the steeper, right side of the track. If desired a frame can be built in the same manner as the original design.

Galileo, whose tracks were a bit rougher than the ones used here, made observations similar to those described in this discussion. Galileo's tracks were made of wood and, as they were sanded smoother, they would operate more efficiently and return the ball to higher positions as the track was tested. Galileo reasoned that friction kept the ball from reaching as high as the starting point. He concluded that the difference between the marble's initial and final heights could be attributed to a force he called friction. He theorized that, without this force, the marble would reach its original height exactly.

Galileo also noticed that changing the steepness of the inclined plane did not affect the marble's movement to its original height. If the slope of the opposite plane were reduced, the marble simply rolled farther to reach its original height. He deduced that if one end of the track were made longer and longer, the ball would simply roll further until it reached its original height. When the track eventually reached the horizontal, the ball would roll on forever. This insight was the basis for the idea of inertia. Simply stated, inertia is an object's resistance to a change in its state of motion.

Additional Activities

Pendulums were also used by Galileo for his demonstrations of mechanical energy. They can oscillate in a smooth back-and-forth transition from potential to kinetic energy, eventually losing out to friction. Many types of pendulums are easy to construct. Consider setting up several and having your students note the similarities.

The shelf bracket material is very cheap and easy to work with. It can be bent into a number of configurations for additional activities.

Prediction Track. Students will enjoy investigating unpredictable patterns with this piece. This track is sloped at either end and has 3 small hills and 4 valleys between the sloped ends. Students should release the ball several times and record the finishing positions. Very small changes in the initial condition of the release give varied results. You can label the rest positions such as "Yes," "No," and "Not Likely" as answers to questions.

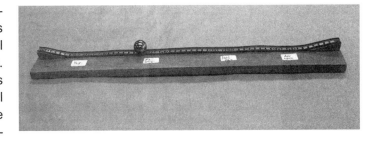

Track Race. In this piece, two tracks have the same initial and finishing position. One track is 25% longer and drops the ball to a lower position in its movement. The ball on this track gains more kinetic energy. The horizontal velocity is greater on the track that dips down and its ball reaches the other side well ahead of the ball on the level track. The balls can be released simultaneously to compare the motions. This is a nice piece with which students can make hypotheses and then compare their predictions to the actual results.

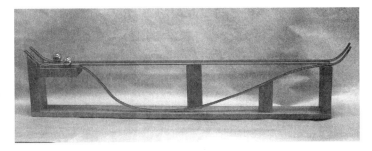

Directions for Assembly

Materials

- 1 shelf bracket, 3 ft. long, available at most hardware stores. (4 ft. and 6 ft. sections are available for longer tracks)

- 6 drywall screws, 1¼ in. long

- 5 screws #4, ½ in. long

- 1 steel ball, ⅝ in. diameter or larger (These are available through hardware stores or science supply companies. Hard plastic, glass, or billiard balls also work well and can be substituted for the steel.)

- 1 wood piece, 3.5 in. × 3 ft.

- 3 wood pieces, 2 in. × 5 in.

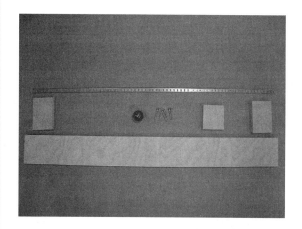

Directions

1. The key to a successful track depends primarily on two factors. The first is having the bracket well supported to eliminate losing energy to vibrations. The second is making sure the bend in the track is not sharp, because this causes the ball to slip or jump off the track. The bend should occur over a 2-inch section of track. Measure in 26 inches from one end and grasp the track in both hands. Gently bend the track to an angle equal to approximately 20 degrees.

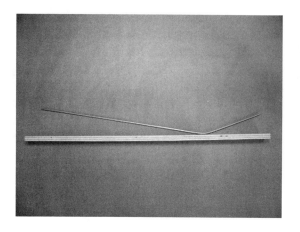

18

2. Both ends of the track must be at the same approximate height. The simplest method is to build one end and then adjust the second end to match it.

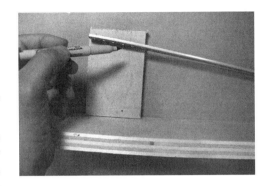

A 3-foot long track should have a height of about 3 to 5 inches. A 4-foot-long track could have a height of about 6 inches. If tracks are made higher, the ball slips on the steeper angle and will lose energy. Place one of the small blocks beside the track and draw a line to match the angle of the track.

SAFETY NOTE

For the next series of instructions, the following safety equipment is strongly recommended:

- Goggles for eye protection. NSTA recommends that you use safety goggles that conform to the ANSI Z87.1 standard and that provide both impact and chemical-splash protection for all science laboratory work.
- Dust mask to guard against breathing in airborne sawdust.
- Gloves whenever power tools are used.

3. Use a saw to cut the pictured angle from the wood block. After cutting the support bracket, sand it smooth and put it back into the correct position on the base.

4. The next step is to anchor the first support to the base. Turn both pieces over and use a pencil to mark two positions for the fastening screws. Most woods will require a pilot hole to be drilled through the bottom of the base into the support bracket.

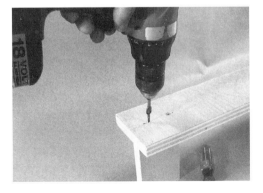

If You Build It, They Will Learn

5. After the pilot holes are drilled; screw the drywall screws through the base into the supports. The heads of each screw must be indented or at least flush with the bottom surface or they may scratch the table surface during use.

6. With the first support bracket firmly attached to the base, match up the end of the track to the edge of the support. Use two small screws to attach the track to the wood base. It may not be necessary to drill pilot holes for these small screws. Check to see that the screws are low enough inside the track so that they will not interfere with the rolling ball.

7. This long section of track can now be anchored to the base itself. Before attaching with screws, check that there are no bends in this portion of the track. Use one or two small screws and screw them through the track into the base. Check screw heads with the metal ball to ensure they are low enough and will not interfere with the movement of the ball.

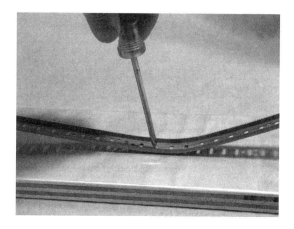

8. Both ends of the track must be at the same height. Use a ruler to measure the height of the first side right at the edge of the track. The other side must be at the same height at the very edge of the track. If the heights do not match, the ball will roll off of the lower side during the demonstration.

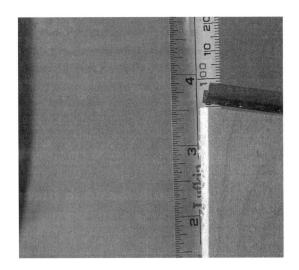

9. Measure the height of the track on the second side; it should match the first side; if it does not match, bend it slightly until it is the same height. Place a wood block against the track.

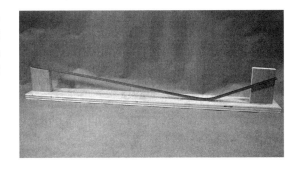

10. Use a pencil to trace the height of the track onto the wood block. Check the height of the track once more before cutting. Remember that this demonstration will not work if the tracks are at different heights. Use a saw to cut the angle into the wood support. After cutting, sand all the edges of this block smooth. This block can be attached to the wood base in the same manner as the first support. Refer back to steps 3, 4, and 5.

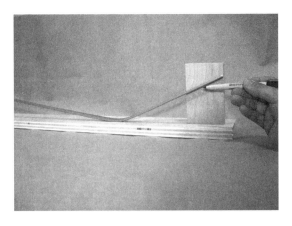

11. To give the track extra stability and reduce vibration, a third block support is needed on the longer side of the track. The location of this support should be about halfway between the support block and the point at which the track is attached directly to the base. Position the third block on the base at this location. Use a pencil to trace the angle onto the block and use a wood saw to cut this angle. Sand the block before attaching it to the wood base.

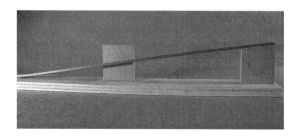

12. To attach this block, position it between the track and base. It should fit snugly but not so tightly that it bends the track or makes the track bulge upward . Grasp the track, block, and base firmly and turn the assembly over. Mark two spots for the screw pilot holes and drill as before. With the assembly turned over, you may find it necessary to prop this section up with some scrap blocks as it is being drilled and secured. Screw in the wood screws to attach the third block.

13. With the base now complete, test the device on a level surface to see how it works. If the track works well, the next step would be to remove the metal track from the base and varnish all wood surfaces.

14. Rub fine sandpaper over all surfaces to remove any rough spots. Signing your name and the date to the underside of the base before varnishing is a nice touch.

   With the wood varnished and dried, reposition the metal track back onto the base supports. Screw the small screws back into the original holes. Check all the small screw heads to ensure they are low enough to not hit the ball during the operation.

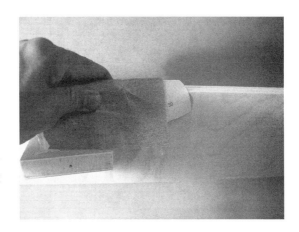

15. Congratulations, your Galileo's track is now complete except for a final smoothing of the rails. Very fine sandpaper should be rubbed against the entire length of both edges of the track to reduce friction between the ball and the track. This is important, because the demonstration is more dramatic if the ball appears to return to the same approximate height as it rolls from one side to the other. A car polish will also help reduce friction and keep the edges from rusting when not in use.

Instructional Information

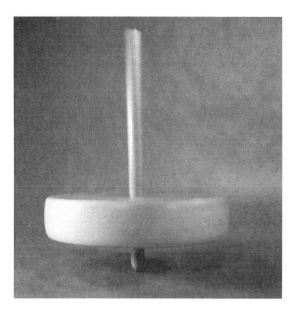 

Overview

Tops are ancient toys that have been spinning around for thousands of years. Their movement, fascinating to watch, appeals to the child in all of us. You can use tops for a very simplistic investigation about spinning objects or a more complex investigation of angular momentum and vector quantities. In either case, ask the question: "Why doesn't it fall over?"

Student Skills

Observation. Students can observe the action of the top and note that its stability is dependent on the speed of rotation. They can also observe the effects of making changes to a homemade top. Students can feel the effect of changing mass by using rulers and lead sinkers in a simple experiment.

Prediction. Students can make predictions of how a top will be affected by changing its mass and dimensions.

Trial and Error. Students can build and then test several theories about the effect of mass, height of the top body, and diameter of the top on the duration of spin.

Measurements. Students can collect data by making tests on the homemade tops in this chapter.

Conclusion. After testing, students can draw conclusions from the data collected in their experiments.

Application. Students can look for similar results in other objects that rotate.

SAFETY NOTE

Pennies taped to the top body may fly off if they are not securely fastened. Students should wear safety glasses in case pennies fly off during testing. NSTA recommends that you use safety goggles that conform to the ANSI Z87.1 standard and that provide both impact and chemical-splash protection for all science laboratory work.

Related Concepts or Processes

Gyroscopes	Rotation kinetic energy
Angular momentum	Rotational inertia
RPMs	Precession
Torque	Center of gravity

Prior Knowledge

The action and the study of the tops appeal to a wide range of age groups. Students in elementary school can use tops as an investigation in changing variables if they understand some very basic concepts of movement and the meaning of *rotation*. Students in the upper elementary grades and older should have an understanding of mass and how to measure it. They should have some practice in testing variables and should be able to interpret results to form conclusions.

Predemonstration Discussion

Before showing the tops, discuss the concepts that will be investigated. The ideas that forces are needed to make an object move and how changing the mass can affect the motion should start the review with students. After students understand those concepts, discuss the movement of rotating objects.

Some questions that can be discussed include the following:
- What is mass?
- What is needed to put an object in motion?
- What is needed to make an object stop?
- What effect does increasing the mass have on the force needed to make an object move?
- What effect does increasing the mass have on the force needed to stop it?
- How does the force need to be applied to make an object rotate?

Suggestions for Presentation

The large top can be used as an introduction to the action of tops. You or your students can spin the large top and some smaller ones while discussing the movement. Have students try to balance the top without spinning and then compare their results to when the top is spinning.

Some questions for discussion include the following:
- Why does a top fall over when you stand it up on its end point?
- What do these tops have in common with each other?
- What are some variables that can be adjusted to make a top spin faster or longer?

Postdemonstration Activities and Discussion

To start an inquiry investigation of tops, divide students into groups of two or three and give them supplies for construction: a short dowel, a thumbtack, an old CD, tape, some cardboard, and several pennies. For students' projects, the small nail is replaced with a thumbtack as the tip of the top. Give students a stopwatch if possible; if not, the second hand on the wall clock will suffice.

Have students wrap tape around the dowel as described in the directions for assembly. They can slide the CD onto the dowel to complete the first trial top. After they spin the top for a few tries, students should discuss and list what variables can be adjusted to make the top spin more efficiently. The cardboard is included in the list in case students wish to make the top body have a larger diameter.

The variables might include:
- Changing the height of the top body
- Changing the mass of the body
- Changing the positions where the mass can be placed
- Changing the diameter of the body

Students should next develop a plan for testing the variables one at a time and decide how they will determine the results. After they have tested all of the variables individually, they should try to combine the best results for each variable to see if a superior top can be produced.

Students can sum up their findings. Some questions that can be used include:
- How did changing the mass affect the spinning time?
- How does changing the size and height of the top body affect the spin time?

The age of your students will determine what other properties should be studied. If you are going to discuss the properties that keep the top from falling over, show some additional examples at this time. Have students list some spinning objects that exhibit

this same behavior. There are many more than they may realize.

You can show a small toy gyroscope and describe it as an advanced type of top. Its action is the same. There are many other types of gyroscopes that serve useful purposes. Students can research the uses for gyroscopes and how they are used. A few examples of uses they may find include navigation and steadying moving vehicles.

Many other devices use rotating bodies as a means of stabilization. For example, try throwing a Frisbee around without the toy rotating. Compare this to when it is thrown correctly, and note the difference.

This stabilization of a rotating body can be shown very nicely using an old 33-1/3 rpm record, a paper clip, and some string. Tie or attach the string to the ceiling, allowing it to hang down to a few feet off the floor. Thread the string through the hole in the record and then tie it to the paper clip. The record will be suspended by the string.

Pull the record and string back like a pendulum and release it. The record will wobble as it swings back and forth a few times.

Try it again, but this time give the record a quick spin as it is released. The record will spin as it swings back and forth. The interesting thing is that it will remain level and stable as it travels back and forth. This demonstration can give students some other ideas where this concept can be applied.

The bicycle wheel is another device to use. With this example, students can feel for themselves the large forces generated by the gyroscopic action. These wheels are available commercially.

An alternative to buying a commercially produced wheel would be to adapt an old bicycle wheel for this purpose. The handles are made from two wooden dowels. Drill holes in the dowels and then fit them over the threads on the wheel's axle.

You might want to use a smaller bicycle wheel, easier for smaller students, when you make your own.

Discussion of Results

The students' investigation should have them test factors that may influence how long the tops will spin. Their results should show that increasing the amount of mass allowed the top to spin for a longer period of time. This increase in mass gives the top additional rotational inertia. Inertia says that an object in motion will continue to keep moving in the same direction unless a force acts on it. It also says that there is a resistance to any change in the movement of an object. The amount of inertia is dependent on mass and increases as the mass of the object is increased.

Rotational inertia is the same idea applied to a spinning object. Once the top is put into motion, the tendency is for it to continue moving in the same direction. As the mass is increased, the resistance to any change of its current movement also increases.

Rotational inertia actually depends on two factors. The first one is the mass; the second one is the distance the mass is located away from the center of rotation. If the mass is placed farther away from the center of rotation, the rotational inertia increases, and the top will spin longer. This concept of changing the distance can be demonstrated to the students using two wooden rulers, some fishing weights, and some tape.

SAFETY NOTE

Use plenty of tape to fasten the sinkers to the rulers. This will minimize the risk of sinkers coming loose and flying off during this experiment. Students should wear safety glasses for eye protection. NSTA recommends that you use safety goggles that conform to the ANSI Z87.1 standard and that provide both impact and chemical-splash protection for all science laboratory work.

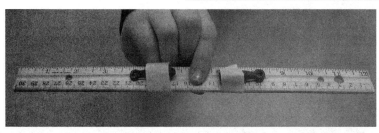

Tape two fishing weights on the inside of the ruler. There should be enough room to fit a finger between the two weights.

Hold the center of the ruler between the thumb and forefinger and then twist it back and forth very rapidly. It is very easy to turn.

Tape two more weights to a second ruler. These should be taped toward the outside of the ruler.

Hold the center of this ruler between the thumb and forefinger and twist it back and forth very rapidly.

The second ruler with the weights nearer the ends is much harder to turn than the first ruler. Not only is this ruler harder to get moving but also, once it is moving, it is harder to stop. This is an example of rotational inertia. It is why the placement of the weight toward the outside of the top body will allow it to spin longer than if the weights were taped near the center.

The interesting thing about the spinning top and other objects is that, once they start spinning, they resist being tipped over. Spinning objects resist any change in the plane of motion. You can feel this very clearly with the toy gyroscope and with the bicycle wheel: They feel as if some invisible force is holding them in place.

The force that you are feeling in the gyroscopes is called *angular momentum.* It is the tendency of a spinning object to keep spinning in the same position until acted on by another force. Angular momentum is the force that keeps a top balanced upright on its point as long as it is spinning. The top will eventually start to slow down due to friction. As the top slows down, it loses this angular momentum. When it loses enough of it, it eventually falls over.

Additional Activities

There is one other process demonstrated by the top as it is spinning. Students may notice the orientation of the axle for the top is usually straight up and down. As the top spins, the axle might have a slight wobble caused by the top body not being perfectly balanced. This wobble is a very quick movement due to the high rate of rotation. Students may also notice that the top axle is slowly turning in small circles as it spins. This action is called *precession.*

Although the explanation of precession is usually too advanced for middle school students, it has not deterred several of them from looking for additional examples.

A classic demonstration of precession may be performed with a bicycle wheel. Try to support a motionless wheel on one side of its axle, and it will fall over as expected. Spin the wheel and support it on one end, and it's an entirely different matter. The wheel will remain upright by rotating around the point of support. The wheel's precession may be shown a few different ways. Support the wheel's axle on a pedestal, momentarily propped on the palm of the hand, or tie a rope to one of the handles and then lift it. The wheel must be spinning fairly quickly for the axle to remain near the horizontal.

Some other objects that can precess as they spin can be researched or investigated. These objects include: toy gyroscopes, Frisbees, boomerangs, spinning coins and plates, bowling balls, tops, and the Earth.

Why should a spinning object act like this? Its motion can be very counterintuitive.

What is actually happening to a top, bicycle wheel, or gyroscope as it rotates might better be illustrated by examining what occurs to different sections of a segmented gyroscope.

This gyroscope wheel is separated into blocks, rather than being a continuous loop, to better illustrate the point. For the sake of simplicity, we will examine a gyroscope of only four blocks. If we examine the motion of and force acting upon the blocks at one moment in time, we gain a better view of what causes precession.

Precession of gyroscopes and tops occurs when one end of the axle is supported and the other end is not. Imagine that the free end of the gyroscope is to pivot freely downward, as intuition tells us it should due to gravity. The blocks on the vertical spokes would follow large arcs that begin at right angles to their initial velocities. The horizontal blocks would follow small arcs that begin in line with their initial velocities.

The top block experiences a force to the left in the image, while the bottom block experiences a force to the right. These forces are unbalanced. The horizontal blocks both experience equal downward force, but in accelerating the falling block and decelerating the rising block, these forces balance, so the horizontal blocks do not contribute to the "twisting" of precession.

Because of the unbalanced forces on the top and bottom blocks, these blocks no longer travel along their original path. The resulting vector is a horizontal velocity that is slightly rotated form the original velocity of the top and the bottom blocks. The gyroscope pictured will rotate out of the page *without falling.* With different blocks constantly being repositioned at the top, bottom, and each position in between, the movement continues to be sideways rather than downward as long as the force on the free side of the axle is applied and the gyroscope remains in motion. This is to say that the gyroscope will precess around the point of support rather than pivot down from it.

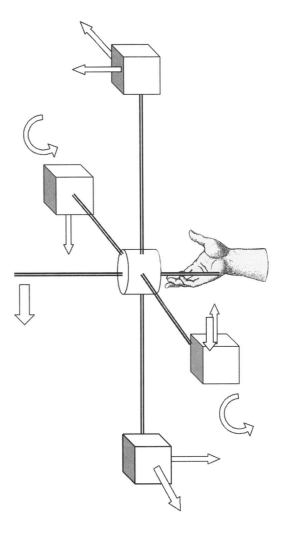

Can You Top This?

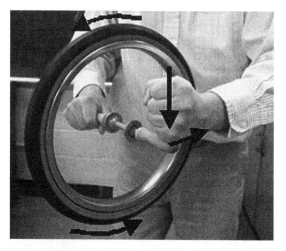

This response can be felt with a spinning bicycle wheel by supporting the wheel's axle on one hand and applying a very quick hit or push down on the free end. The wheel will respond with a sideways movement rather than a movement downward as shown in the bottom picture. Newton's first law of motion can help explain precession. If the gyroscope were not spinning it would fall over. If the gyroscope is spinning, Newton's first law of motion states that a body in motion continues to move at a constant speed along a straight line unless acted upon by an unbalanced force.

The block on top of the gyroscope is acted on by the force applied to the axle and begins to move toward the left. It continues trying to move leftward because of Newton's first law of motion, but the gyroscope's spinning rotates it to a new position. The blocks on the bottom of the gyroscope are trying to do just the opposite and move toward the right and are also moved to a new position. This effect is the cause of precession. With different blocks constantly being repositioned at the top, bottom, and each position in between, the movement continues to be sideways rather than downward as long as the force on the free side of the axle is applied and the gyroscope remains in motion.

This piece uses a wooden hub cut out of a scrap piece of 2-inch x 4-inch stud. It has 16 blocks or balls extending out as points of the rim. Wooden dowels act as spokes to hold the blocks in place. The hub has two bearings that fit into it. The bearings were removed from a skateboard wheel assembly.

Two different sized holes are drilled through the center of the hub. The sizes will depend on the available bearing and axle size. The outer hole is a tight fit for the bearing diameter. The inner hole through the hub allows the small axle to pass through it.

The axle that fits through the bearing is made from a wooden dowel. You can slide it through the holes with a little effort. You can wrap rubber bands on the dowel to help hold the axle position on the hub.

The segmented gyroscope can hang on a cord and precess around the support.

A simpler model with 8 spokes and no bearings could be used for explanation purposes. It is simpler to build and can be used for demonstrating precession conceptually. It can be spun like a top but cannot be hung from a cord to revolve around the support: This requires an axle that can turn freely on bearings.

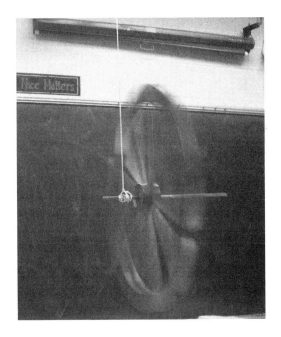

Directions for Assembly

Wood Version

Materials

- 1 wooden dowel, ½ in. diameter × 10 in. long
- 1 scrap of wood, 2 in. × 8 in. or 2 in. × 10 in. × 1 ft. long

Many designs and variations are available for making tops. This piece is used because its large size makes it ideal for demonstration and because it is easy to construct.

Directions

1. Start by making the body of the top. Use a compass to draw the circumference on the wood. The size of the top can be adjusted to fit the piece of scrap wood available. The one pictured in this book has a diameter of about 9 inches.

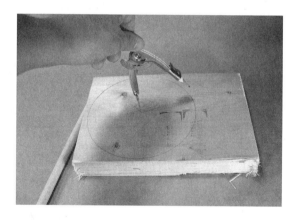

SAFETY NOTE

While completing the wood base, the following safety equipment is strongly suggested:

Goggles for eye protection. NSTA recommends that for all science laboratory work you use safety goggles that conform to the ANSI Z87.1 standards and that provide both impact and chemical-splash protection.

Dust mask to guard against breathing in airborne sawdust

Gloves whenever power tools are used

2. Use a saw to cut out the body of the top. Try to cut the body out as accurately and smoothly as possible to reduce the amount of sanding that will be required.

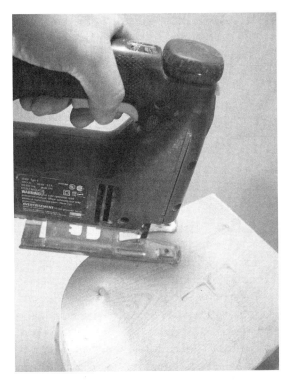

3. Drill a hole through the body of the top. This hole should be the same diameter as the wooden dowel. One-half inch dowels work very nicely, but other sizes will do.

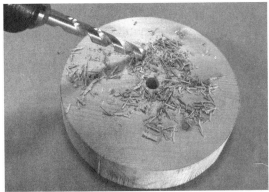

4. Before gluing the dowel permanently into the top body, insert it into the body and try spinning it at various heights. After finding the desirable height for the top body, apply a small amount of glue into the hole drilled and then insert the dowel to the desired depth. Allow the glue to dry overnight.

5. Use a sander or hand sand the body and the dowel smooth. Round off the bottom of the dowel.

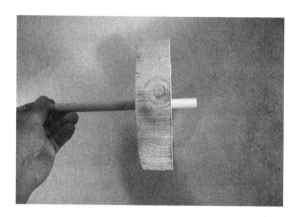

6. The body of the top must be balanced for it to spin smoothly. Set two scraps of wood or 2 matching books standing on their ends about 3 inches apart. Lay the top on the edges of the 2 pieces using the dowel as an axle. Rotate the top about one-half turn and release it. If the top is unbalanced, the heavy side will turn to the bottom. Tape 1 or 2 wood screws to the topside of the top and spin the top a half turn. Add or subtract the number of screws until the top is balanced.

7. Drill pilot holes and then screw in the number of wood screws needed to balance the top according to the balancing trials. The screws should be set beneath the level of the wood.

8. Cover the top of the screw heads with a small amount of wood filler and allow it to dry. Sand all the edges, body, and dowels of the top with medium and then fine grit sandpaper. Paint the top with one or two coats of varnish and then allow it to dry thoroughly.

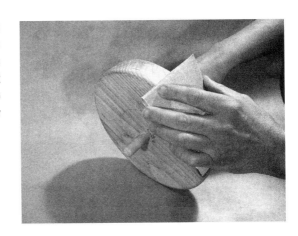

9. To spin the top, grasp it between the palms of both hands and then rapidly push one hand forward and the other backward. The top should spin between your hands. With a little practice, you can make the top spin very quickly by repeating this motion several times as it spins.

10. You can try other sizes and variations after mastering the basics. Changing mass, location, and other variables may yield better results with some trial and error.

Student Model

Materials

- 1 wooden dowel, ½ in. diameter × 3 in. long
- 5 discarded CDs or pieces of cardboard
- 1 finishing nail, size #2
- 15 pennies
- 1 roll of plastic or masking tape

Directions

1. Constructing these tops requires little effort and a minimal use of tools. To start, cut a ½-inch dowel into 3 4-inch lengths, depending on number of tops you want. Sand any rough edges smooth.

   Drill a $\frac{1}{16}$-inch pilot hole into the center of the diameter of the wood dowel. Then use the hammer to drive a small nail into this hole about halfway. This will serve as the tip of the top.

   As an alternative to the nail, a thumbtack can be used. Push it into the dowel about halfway.

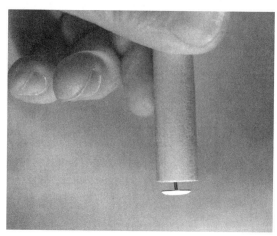

2. Since the dowels are a bit too narrow to hold the CD discs tight enough without wobbling, wrap 3 or 4 lengths of tape around the shaft of the wood dowel at the appropriate height for the top body.

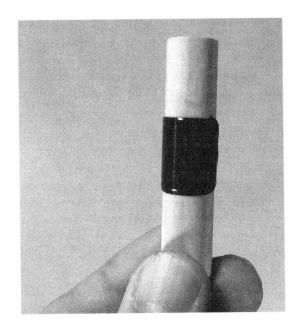

3. You can then slide a CD disk can onto the dowel to make the body of the top. Enough tape should be added to ensure a tight fit between the dowel and the CD. Adding 3 or 4 CDs will give the body more mass, and the top will spin for longer periods of time.

You can tape pennies around the circumference of the top CD to give the top additional mass. The number and placement of the pennies can be variables for students to adjust. They may want to try several combinations to find the optimal spin time.

SAFETY NOTE
Use adequate amounts of tape to reduce the chances of pennies coming loose and flying off as the top is spinning. Safety glasses should be worn. NSTA recommends that you use safety goggles that conform to the ANSI Z87.1 standards and that provide both impact and chemical-splash protection for all science laboratory work.

If you do not have enough CDs, use cardboard for the top body. There are a few advantages to the cardboard. One is the price; the other is that cardboard allows for a larger diameter on the top body.

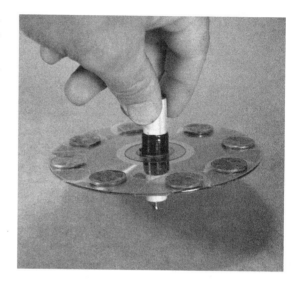

This student's top spun for more than 5 minutes.

Instructional Information

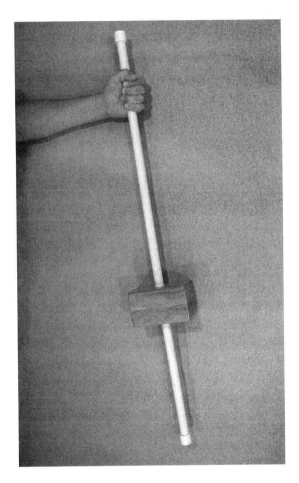 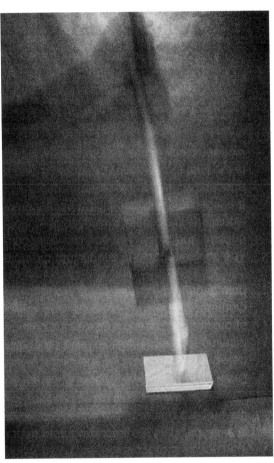

Overview

Newton's first law of motion describes the resistance of an object to a change in the speed and direction of its motion. The law also holds that objects will resist being put into motion. This concept is described as inertia, and both aspects of the law can be demonstrated using this device, which is a heavy block with a hole through the center and one end of a plastic tube inserted into the hole. To demonstrate it, you will use a rubber hammer and hit the other end of the plastic tube with a succession of blows, causing the block to move toward the direction of the hammer with each blow. To show the second aspect of inertia, slide the block near the top of the tube. Hold the tube and block above a tabletop and move it rapidly toward this surface. When the tube strikes the table, it will stop, but the block will slide a short distance down the tube toward the table.

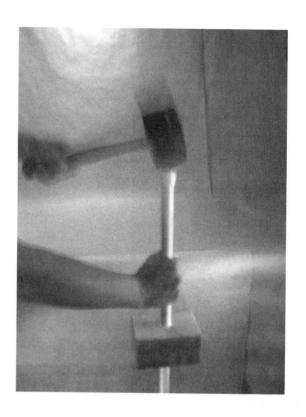

Student Skills

Observation. Students can observe the action of the block when it is put into motion and the resistance to motion as the pipe is given swift taps by a hammer.
Research. Students can research the concept of inertia and its applications.
Application. Students should be able to identify and demonstrate many examples that illustrate the concept of inertia.

Related Concepts or Processes

Inertia

Force

Mass

Newton's first law of motion

Impulse

Friction

Balanced and unbalanced forces

Acceleration

Prior Knowledge

This device can be used to introduce or to reinforce the concept of inertia. In either case, students should understand some fundamental processes that apply to this demonstration. One concept is that force is applied as a push or a pull against an object, and forces are required to produce motion. Students should also have some ideas about friction as a resistance to motion. And, although students may not have been introduced formally to Newton's second law, they most likely have a basic intuitive understanding that there is a relationship among the amount of force applied, the mass of an object, and its acceleration.

Predemonstration Discussion

Any discussion before the demonstration should center on force, motion, and friction. Students should understand why an object accelerates or decelerates. Review with them that any change in velocity occurs because of an unbalanced force that is opposite to the velocity of the object.

Questions to discuss could include the following:
- Why do objects move?
- Can objects ever move by themselves?
- What are some types or examples of objects that can move by themselves? How do these objects accomplish this?
- What are some types or examples of objects that cannot move by themselves? What is needed to put these objects in motion?
- What is the result of balanced forces?
- What is the result of unbalanced forces?
- What happens to the motion of an object when a force stops being applied to it?
- What is it that causes an object to slow down?

Suggestions for Presentation

If students have no previous experience with inertia and Newton's first law of motion, they can learn the concept as you demonstrate the device. If you use good questioning techniques, the students can determine for themselves what the principle or concept is that is being demonstrated. If students already have an understanding of Newton's law, then you can use this piece to review the concept. Newton's law is described in two parts: The first part predicts the behavior of stationary objects, and the second predicts the behavior of moving objects.

Part One

Start with the block located somewhere near the middle of the tube. Using a bit of showmanship, exaggerate the force needed and slide the block to that position. Show this action to the students, giving them a visual cue that the block can move on the tube. Wave the block and tube up in the air and gently move the block forward and backward showing that the block has enough friction on the tube that it does not slide easily.

Inertia Block

Hold the tube vertically with the block at the bottom end and your hand near the top of the tube. Use a rubber mallet or similar soft object to hit the top end cap with quick successive blows. The block will slowly climb up the tube and eventually reach your hand. As you hit the top of the tube, try not to hold the tube too rigidly, but rather allow it to move in small increments from the hammer blows.

The orientation of the demonstration can be changed. Try the same process holding the device sideways or upside down.

Interactive questions during presentation could include the following:
- Which is easier to move, an object with only a small mass or one that has a lot of mass?
- What is needed to make an object move?
- My hand is holding the tube, but what happens to the tube as I hit it?
- If the stick is moved a short quick distance when I hit it, is the block moving also?
- If I were to hit the stick harder, how might this affect the distance the tube moves through the block?
- Do you think it would make a difference if we held this tube in another direction such as sideways or upside down? Why would we need fewer blows if we tried this upside down or sideways?

Part Two

To demonstrate the second part of Newton's law of motion, the block should be positioned at an end of the tube. Hold the tube vertically with the block positioned at the top end of the tube. Holding the tube above a tabletop, swing it straight down and have the bottom end of the tube strike a hard surface such as the tabletop or the floor. The purpose is to stop the tube very abruptly. The block will slide down the tube for a short distance. Repeating this step will drive the block downward with each successive blow; the distance the block moves with each blow will depend on the speed of the swinging movement and the amount of friction between the blocks and the tube. The orientation of the demonstration can be changed. Try the same procedure with the tube held sideways and strike the tube against a wall. This can even be tried with the assembly moving upward if there is a suitable surface to hit. My preferred location is swinging upward in the doorway and hitting the top of the door frame.

Interactive questions during presentation could include the following:
- After the block is put into motion, and the tube stops, what direction does the block continue to travel toward?
- Is it gravity that makes the block move down the tube?
- Why does the block move part way down the tube?
- What is causing the block to stop?

- If I were to swing the block and tube down faster, how might this affect the distance the block moves down the tube?
- Do you think it would make a difference if we were to move the block and tube in another direction such as sideways or upside down?
- Why would we need more blows if we tried this going upward instead of down?

Postdemonstration Activities and Discussion

A few writing prompts and ideas to research might include the following:
- How would either part of this demonstration change if the block had more mass or less mass?
- The block and tube are in motion; how would this experiment change if there were more friction between the block and tube?
- The block and tube are in motion; how would this experiment change as we decreased the amount of friction between the block and tube?
- How would the experiment change if there were no friction between the block and tube?
- What direction and how far would the block travel if there were no friction to stop it?
- Inertia is a favorite topic in most science classrooms and can be demonstrated in a variety of ways. Have students research other examples and perform additional demonstrations.
- Have students draw up two separate lists of ordinary occurrences that demonstrate part one or part two of Newton's law of inertia.
- Students can research the lives of Galileo and Newton.
- Students can research the reasons why seat belts and air bags are used in cars.

Additional Activities

There are many good examples for demonstrating Newton's first law of motion.

One of the best known is yanking a tablecloth from under a setting of plates and glasses on a table. Unfortunately, this demonstration has a high rate of failure when the tablecloth has a hem. The dishes and glasses get caught by the hem and fall over. You can try it using a large sheet of paper instead of the tablecloth.

One of the simplest and most effective demonstrations for showing inertia can be done with a heavy weight and a thin piece of string or thread. Fasten the string to the block, either by tying it into a hook or around the block.

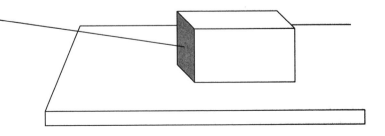

The string can be pulled slowly and the block will move. What will happen if the string is pulled very quickly? The block will resist accelerating and the string will break, following Newton's first law, part one.

If the block is put into motion and the thread is used to try to stop the block, the thread will break and the block will keep sliding for a short distance. This demonstration is an example of the second part of Newton's first law.

Students can try making their own version of the inertia block using a ¼-inch-diameter wood dowel and a piece of vegetable or fruit such as an apple. They should push the stick through the core of the apple and then follow the same directions given for the device.

Directions for Assembly

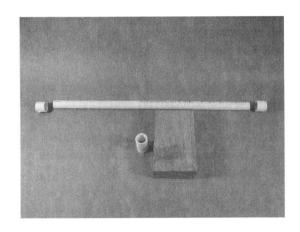

Inertia Block

Materials

- 1 wooden block, 4 in. × 4 in., thickness may vary from 2 in. to 6 in. due to available materials

- epoxy glue

- wood varnish

- 1 PVC pipe, ½ in. diameter × 3 feet

- 2 PVC end caps for ½ in. pipe

- 1 PVC coupler for ½ in. pipe

SAFETY NOTE

For this series of instructions, the following safety equipment is strongly recommended:

- Goggles for eye protection. NSTA recommends that you use safety goggles that conform to the ANSI Z87.1 standard and that provide both impact and chemical-splash protection for all science laboratory work.
- Dust mask to guard against breathing in airborne sawdust.
- Gloves whenever power tools are used.

Directions

1. The effectiveness of this demonstration depends on the block having sufficient mass. Hardwoods such as oak or maple will work better than pine. The wooden block dimensions should be approximately 4 inches by 4 inches by 2 or more inches. If thin wood is available, glue the pieces together to get the proper thickness.

   Draw lines from each opposing corner to determine the center of the block. After locating the center, use a wood bit that is approximately the same size as the outside diameter of the PVC couplers and drill a hole through the center of the block.

2. The coupler should fit snugly into the hole drilled in the block. The end cap will occasionally hit this coupler during the operation. It will become dislodged if it is not securely attached within the block. If the connector is too tight to push in by hand, tap it with a wooden block to push it into place.

3. If the drilled hole is not quite large enough, sand the inside of the drilled hole until it is the right size. To do so, wrap a piece of sandpaper around a wooden dowel and use a rubber band to hold it in place. This sanding stick can be used with the drill to sand the inside of the block. Use the drill on high speed to get a smooth, rounded hole.

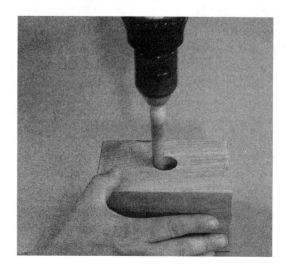

4. If the block is more than ½ inch thicker than the coupler, use a small handsaw to cut the PVC connector in half so that you have 2 rings. You will set 1 piece of the connector into each side of the block. If the block is large enough, 2 whole couplers can be used.

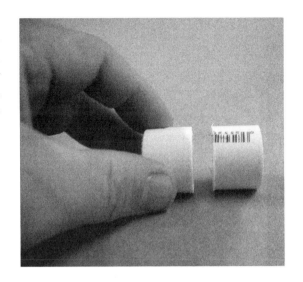

5. Before the coupler is glued inside the block, there is a ring of plastic inside the connector that you need to sand off. Use the sandpaper wrapped around the dowel rod to sand the inside of the ring until the coupler can slide all the way through the PVC pipe with effort. Do not sand off too much: There must be some friction between the coupler and the pipe. If the fitting is too loose, the block will move on its own when the pipe is held vertically. Using the dowel on the drill is faster than sanding by hand.

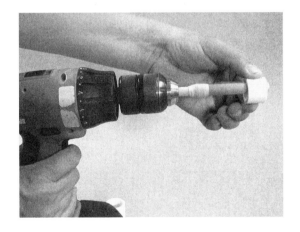

6. If there is only 1 coupler to fit into the wooden block, apply some epoxy glue to the inside of the block and press the coupler into place and allow it to dry. If the connector is a tight fit, use a piece of wood to tap it into place.

If you use more than 1 coupler, they will need to be glued into place one at a time. Start by gluing 1 half of the connector into 1 side of the wood.

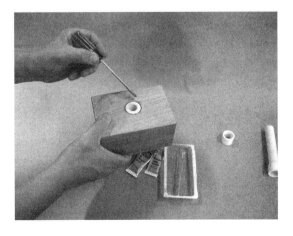

7. Make sure that the edge of the coupler is flush with the block surface. Try to remove as much of the wet glue as possible before it dries on the wood surface. It is easy to remove glue while it is wet but not after it dries.

8. If 2 coupler pieces are needed, insert a piece of PVC piping through both couplers while gluing the second piece in place. This will help ensure they are aligned properly. Glue the other half of the coupler into the opposite side of the block. Once again make sure that the edge of the coupler is flush with the wooden surface.

   Sand the block to remove all traces of glue around the connector. If the coupler was not glued flush with the wood surface, the excess can also be sanded away.

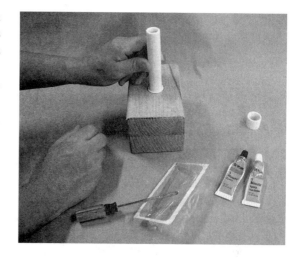

9. After the glue has dried, the block should slide on the tube with some effort. If it is too hard to move the block, it can be made easier by sanding the inside of the PVC coupler. Do not make it too easy, or the demonstration will not work. Varnish the block to seal the wood and give it a nicer appearance.

10. The PVC piping usually comes with writing on it. Washing the PVC pipe with hot soapy water and scrubbing with a scouring pad can remove this and give the piece a nicer appearance.

   With the block on the tube, slide the end caps over each end of the tube. It is not necessary to glue the caps on.

11. The completed project.

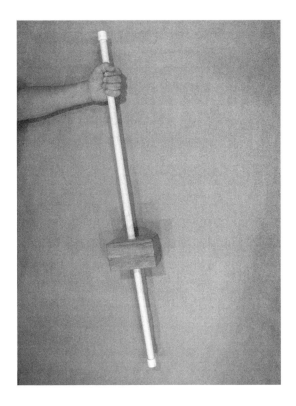

Instructional Information

Overview

Examples of resonance can be shown very nicely by using a variety of pendulum demonstrations. The first device shown is a coupled pendulum. It has two simple pendulums hanging from a common cross-support string. When one pendulum is set into motion, the gentle nudges from the support string slowly transfers the energy into the second pendulum as the first pendulum slows down and stops. The process reverses and then repeats itself back and forth between the two pendulums until they both eventually stop. The second example is a Wilberforce pendulum. If you lift the spring bob a short distance and release it, the spring and weight will oscillate vertically for a few movements. As the weighted spring continues to oscillate up and down, its motion will change completely into torsion or twisting motion within 6 to 10 movements. As it continues, the pendulum will change back and forth from one type of movement to the other until it eventually stops.

Student Skills

Prediction. Students can list all the possible effects that one pendulum may have on the other and predict the most likely outcome.

Observation. Students can observe the behavior of the pendulum for several complete transfers of energy and note that system eventually slows down and stops.

Draw a Conclusion. After observing the motion of the coupled pendulums or the Wilberforce pendulum, students can draw conclusions about the flow of energy through a system.

Application. Students should be able to identify a variety of other situations in which energy transfers due to resonance, such as a child swinging.

Trial and Error. Students can make several changes in variables to observe the effect on the system (change of one or both masses, tightness of support string, change length of one or both strings). Students can try adjusting the positions of the masses on the Wilberforce pendulum.

Communication. Students can express their understanding to others through drawings and written explanations.

Related Concepts or Processes

Simple harmonic motion	Potential energy
Pendulums	Kinetic energy
Resonance	Amplitude
Oscillation	Resonant frequency
Principles of dynamics	Hooke's law

Prior Knowledge

The coupled pendulum may be appropriate for students from fifth grade and up. It is helpful while students are learning about energy systems and energy transfer. Students should have some basic understanding of and be able to identify types of energy and their uses. They should know that simple objects such as pendulums can be given potential energy motion that will turn into kinetic and then back into potential several times during its operation. Students should also have been exposed to a basic understanding of simple harmonic motion as displayed by objects that vibrate or oscillate back and forth. The Wilberforce pendulum is very interesting in its movement, but younger students may find it difficult to understand how and why the pendulum changes from one type of movement into another.

Predemonstration Discussion

Coupled Pendulum

This experiment will not be successful unless students understand what a pendulum is and how it works. Questions for discussion prior to demonstration should focus on pendulum movements and energy. They can include the following:

* How do we apply energy to a simple pendulum?

- What happens to the velocity of the bob on the downward movement toward a rest position?
- How does the velocity differ as it passes the rest position and climbs upward?
- Will the pendulum reach the same height on the other side of the movement as it had at the starting point?
- Why does a pendulum lose energy after several movements and where does it go?
- What similarities can the up and down movement of a weight on a spring have with a simple pendulum swinging back and forth?

Wilberforce Pendulum

Before showing the Wilberforce pendulum, have students examine the movement of a spring pendulum. A simple spring and weight can show the basics of Hooke's law as it is applied to pendulums. You should point out that, when many spring pendulums oscillate up and down, the weight will twist during the movement. This can be noticeable in larger coiled springs but is a very slight movement in smaller tightly coiled springs. A piece of tape on a round weight will help to illustrate the twisting movement during the vertical oscillations. It is more interesting to replace the rounded weight with another object with which rotation can be seen more easily, perhaps a set of wrenches that are attached to different-sized springs. When the springs oscillate up and down, a twisting or torsional movement is also evident. The torsional motion varies with the size of the coil and the cross-sectional area of the spring material.

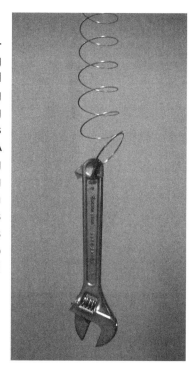

You can show a torsional pendulum before using the Wilberforce pendulum. If one is not available, it can be made with a hacksaw blade, a 12-inch-long block of wood, and a C-clamp. The block of wood is attached perpendicular to the length of the hacksaw blade with a screw. The other end is attached to a support block with a screw or a small clamp. The support block is attached to a table with a C-clamp. Twist the block and release to make it oscillate as a torsional pendulum.

If You Build It, They Will Learn

Suggestions for Presentation

Coupled Pendulum

Before starting the coupled pendulum experiment, make sure that both pendulums are the same length and positioned an equal distance from the end supports. Next have someone gently pull back on one of the pendulums and let it go. It should begin to swing back and forth. After a few oscillations, students should be able to notice that the other pendulum has begun to move, picking up speed and amplitude with each swing. The first pendulum that moved will decrease its amplitude with each swing and eventually stop, leaving the second pendulum briefly swinging by itself. This whole process begins to reverse, and soon the first pendulum is swinging again while the second one is stopped. The energy will repeatedly transfer the motion back and forth between them this way as long as they continue to swing. After discussing the movement and energy transfer of this system, try pulling both of the pendulums back and release them together. They will swing back and forth together as long as this system has energy.

Interactive questions during the presentation could include the following:
- What characteristics do the pendulums have in common?
- What will happen if one of the pendulums is pulled back and released?
- What do you notice occurring within the system as pendulums continue to swing back and forth?
- What will eventually happen to the energy in this system?
- What do you think will happen if both pendulums are pulled back and released together?
- If you look very closely, what can you see happening to the support bars during the movement of the pendulums?

Wilberforce Pendulum

Set out the Wilberforce pendulum for students to examine. Ask a student to carefully lift the mass and then drop it a short distance. Say that you do not want the mass to twist as it falls. After several attempts, students will observe that the mass of the pendulum cannot be kept from twisting after a few oscillations. After watching it for an extended period of time, students can observe that the oscillations repeatedly change from one type of movement into the other.

Interactive questions during the presentation could include the following:
- What happens to the weight of a spring pendulum after several oscillations?
- Describe your observations of the Wilberforce pendulum.
- Is it possible to keep the pendulum from rotating as it moves up and down?
- What is a torsional movement?
- What must the spring be doing as it stretches and compresses?

- How does the movement change if the weights are repositioned on the dowel?
- If the weights are moved towards the center, does the torsional oscillation increase or decrease?

Postdemonstration Activities and Discussion

Students can set up their own coupled pendulums by suspending a string from the edges of two desks or tables. Use two fishing weights or other available materials for the bobs.

Have students design some additional variables to try with the coupled pendulum. Activities can include the following:
- Changing the length of both strings
- Changing the length of one string
- Changing the mass of both bobs
- Doubling the mass of one bob
- Changing the distance between the bobs

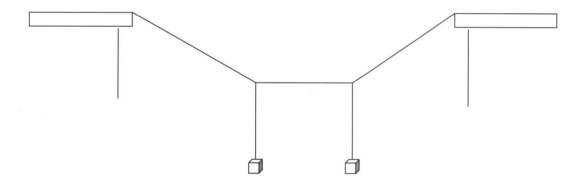

Students can set up their own Wilberforce pendulum using a dowel rod, a coiled spring toy, duct tape, and a ruler. The instructions for construction are at the end of this section. Activities for investigation could include the following:
- changing the amount of spring that may stretch
- noting what happens to the period of the vertical oscillation
- noting what happens to the distances the masses need to be moved on the dowel to get the oscillations to match again
- changing the amount of clay used for the masses
- noting what happens to the period of the vertical oscillation

If a playground swing is pulled from its rest position and released, it begins to oscillate like a pendulum. This oscillation has its own natural time period and is easily measured. Each time the swing moves forward and then returns to its starting position counts as one cycle. Using a stopwatch, determine the length of time a swing needs to complete, say, 10 cycles. Divide 10 cycles by the time and you have the swing's period, the time needed for 1 oscillation. A typical swing might take 6 seconds to complete 1 oscillation.

If someone stands behind a child on a swing and pushes periodically, it becomes a forced vibration with energy being transferred to the child and swing; every push causes the child to go higher and higher. This forced vibration is another example of resonance.

The forced vibration can also be caused by the child on the swing. Children usually start by pushing off of the ground at regular intervals. When children do not push off the ground, they can move themselves by shifting their center of mass very slightly. They change their center of mass by the position of their legs or torso. This creates a slight pushing force which can make the swing go higher and higher. The large amplitude is caused by small forces applied over and over again, either from outside the system or from within the system, but each must be applied at the correct time.

Suggested activity. Although taking a whole science class to visit a playground may not be possible, take a few volunteers of various sizes to a playground, or, if students are mature enough, ask a few to perform the following.

Take a video recorder to the playground and record several variations of the movement of a swing set. The first sequence can be a student on the swing being pushed by someone standing behind the student on the swing. Instruct the student on the swing to keep his or body in the same position and not to "help" by moving body parts. The movement should start from rest and the amplitude would slowly be increased. The pushing can cease and the oscillations will decrease in size, or pushes can be applied at the "wrong" time causing the decrease in oscillation amplitude. Additional sequences to be recorded might include the following:
- the oscillation of an empty swing
- the oscillation of a small person on a swing
- the oscillation of a large person on a swing

- having a person sit on a motionless swing and extend the legs forward out and hold.
- having a person sit on a motionless swing and lean back and hold
- having a person demonstrate "swinging" by shifting arms, legs, and leaning backward
- having a person demonstrate "swinging" by shifting of legs only
- having a person demonstrate "swinging" by leaning backwards with the torso, while the legs remain fixed
- having a person try to achieve a predetermined height as quickly as possible
- having a person demonstrate how to slow themselves down after a fixed height is reached

Interactive questions for discussion could include the following:
- How do you think the applied force changes when comparing the empty swing to the small person on the swing or to the large person on a swing?
- Is it possible for a child to push an adult on a swing?
- Where is the center of gravity located for a person sitting on a swing?
- What happens to the center of gravity if a person extends his or her legs or torso?
- When should a push be applied to increase the amplitude of a swing?
- What happens if someone stops pushing?
- What happens if a push is applied at the "wrong time"?
- If a person to push is not available, how can children swing themselves?
- When does a person shift body weight to achieve the maximum gain in amplitude?
- How does the body position change as the swing is descending on a swing movement?
- How does the body position change as the swing is ascending on a swing movement?
- How does a child alter his or her movements to get the swing to stop?

A similar way of showing that resonance is dependent on applying forces at the correct time is by using an empty metal paint can, some weights, a magnet, and some string. Hang the can from the ceiling so it will act as the pendulum bob. Put some weights inside the can and add a towel to keep the weights from moving around inside the can. The amount of weight to add will depend on magnet strength.

Stick the magnet to the side of the can with an additional string attached to it. The trick is to pull on the magnet string in intervals that will increase the amplitude of the can's swing. If students pull too hard or at the wrong time, the magnet will detach itself. When they pull at the correct times, the can will slowly increase the size of the movement until the movement becomes quite large.

Some points to investigate include the following:
- finding out what happens if you pull too hard
- pulling to increase the amplitude of the swing
- slowing the can down by applying pressure at the "wrong" time after the oscillations are large
- removing some weight from the can and repeating the experiment
- adding additional weight to the can and repeating the experiments

Pendulums have played an important role in the history of mechanical physics, both in the theoretical and practical definition of equal periods of time. Students may be interested in researching the story of how Galileo sat in church and discovered that a pendulum could sweep out equal units of time. The church is said to be the Cathedral of Pisa, with its famous leaning bell tower, another location at which Galileo is said to have performed science experiments. He reportedly dropped different-sized balls from the tower and had observers note the positions of the balls relative to each other as they fell.

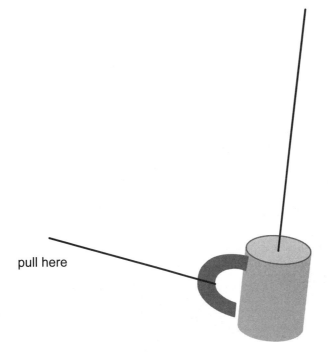

pull here

Discussion of Results

Coupled Pendulum

The resonance of these two bobs on the coupled pendulum are characterized by a continuous exchange of energy from one to the other.

Three cases are particularly interesting to observe:
1. One of the two pendulums is initially at rest. In this case, the swing of the second moving pendulum is absorbed by the first until it is totally stopped, at

which point the first reaches its maximum. Then the situation is reversed, and so on.
2. The two pendulums have the same movement—they are in phase.
3. The two pendulums are initially in opposite positions—they are out of phase.

Any other movement can be described as a combination of the two last cases.

The energy exchange in these systems begins with both pendulums having the same length and thus having the same matching frequency. Every time the first pendulum swings, the connecting string gives the second pendulum a small tug, making it swing also. Because the second pendulum has the same frequency as the first, the tug occurs in a position that adds to the movement of the second pendulum. This can be compared to a person pushing a child on a swing. Small pushes accumulate to a very large amplitude.

The tugging of one pendulum on the other occurs because the pendulums swing slightly out of phase with each other. The second pendulum's movement lags behind the movement of the first pendulum. As soon as the second pendulum starts to swing, it starts pulling back on the first pendulum. These pulls are applied at the wrong place in the first pendulum movement, so the effect is additive. The result is that the first pendulum slows down. This can be compared to a person pushing someone on a swing at the wrong time: The push will interfere with the swing movement and become smaller rather than larger.

Eventually, the first pendulum comes to rest. It has transferred all of its energy to the second pendulum. The original situation is exactly reversed with the first pendulum motionless and all of the energy now within the second pendulum. The process repeats itself with the two pendulums reversing roles until eventually all of the energy is removed from the system.

Wilberforce Pendulum

When the Wilberforce pendulum is adjusted properly, the energy of the pendulum flows back and forth between the two types of oscillations. One type of oscillation is called *translational* (up and down movement); the other type is called *rotational* (a back and forth twisting motion around the center axis). By moving the blocks in toward the center or toward the outside, the moment of inertia of the masses can be changed. If the blocks are moved toward the center, the moment of inertia becomes less, so the rotational movement becomes faster. When the blocks are moved toward the outside, the moment of inertia is increased and the rotational movement is slower. To get a complete transfer of energy from one type of oscillation to the other, both frequencies must exactly match. Move the weights in or out to adjust the rotational frequency until it matches the translational frequency.

A spring pendulum rotates because slight torsional twisting motions are introduced by the contraction and stretching of the spring. This can be shown on a spring pendulum as it oscillates up and down. Ideally, the two frequencies match on a Wilberforce pendulum. The resonance is the accumulation of the twisting movement until all of the energy is directed into a rotational oscillation. The rotational movement will then change back into translational movement over the next few oscillations. This happens because, as the spring rotates in the direction that tightens the spring coil, the blocks are lifted upward. As the spring rotates in the opposite direction, the coil unwinds, allowing the blocks to fall downward. The next couple of oscillations increase this change until all of the rotational movement is changed back into a translational movement.

Additional Activities

Another example of resonance can be shown with two matching tuning forks mounted on top of wooden hollow boxes. Two cigar boxes work well. Remove the top and one of the sides of each box. Drill a small hole into the middle of the bottom. Make sure the forks are a tight fit into each of these holes and held there by friction between the base of the tuning the box.

Strike one of the forks and a sympathetic vibration will make the second tuning fork vibrate as well.

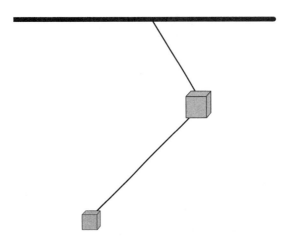

For those interested in further studies, many other fascinating examples can be reproduced in the classroom. Some are quite easy, like the one shown. Tie a string to a support; add a weight to the string, and add a second weight further down the string. You can tune the pendulums by adjusting the positions of the weights on the string. The results give some very chaotic examples of resonance with the weights responding in some very unpredictable movements.

Directions for Assembly

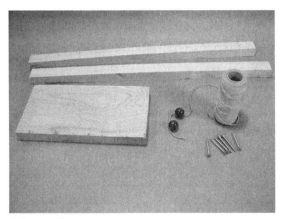

Coupled Pendulum
Materials

- 1 block of wood, 1 × 6 × 10 in.
- 2 strips of wood, 1 × 1 × 20 in.
- 2 drilled steel balls or fishing weights
- 6 wood screws, 1½ in. long
- nylon string

Directions

1. The base and height of the coupled pendulum can be varied according to the available materials. The type of string, length of the pendulum, or the mass of the weights can also be varied.

SAFETY NOTE

For this series of instructions, the following safety equipment is strongly recommended:

- Goggles for eye protection. NSTA recommends that you use safety goggles that conform to the ANSI Z87.1 standard and that provide both impact and chemical-splash protection for all science laboratory work.
- Dust mask to guard against breathing in airborne sawdust.
- Gloves whenever power tools are used.

2. The first pieces that are needed are the vertical supports. The measurements for the supports are 1 inch by 1 inch with a length of about 20 to 24 inches. Cut the two supports and make sure they are the same length. Using a saw, cut a ½-inch-long groove into the top of each support for holding the string.

3. Fit the string into the groove cut into the top of the two vertical supports.

4. The next step is the production of the base. The bottom of this piece is 6 inches by 10 inches. The base needs to be heavy enough to keep it stable. A hardwood is preferred, but if pine is used, glue 2 pieces together to double the thickness or use a piece that is 2 inches thick.

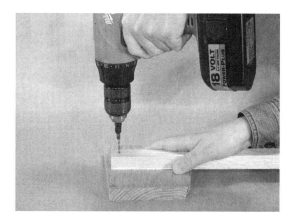

5. The bottom of each vertical support should have 2 or 3 pilot holes drilled into it for the wood screws. Place a piece of scrap wood under the wood before drilling.

6. Sand all 3 pieces of wood before assembling the base.

7. Measure the shorter sides of the base to find the middle of each side. These positions will be used for the placement of each vertical support. Place the first vertical support against the middle of the wood base. Use the drill bit to continue the first of the holes from the support into the wood base.

8. Screw in the first wood screw connecting the support to the base. Check the support to make sure it is vertical and in the correct position before drilling the second hole and attaching the second screw.

9. Use a carpenter's square to make sure the supports are straight up from the base. If they are not straight, adjust them to the correct position and add a third screw to lock them in place.

   After completing the first vertical support bar, follow the same procedure for the opposite side of the base.

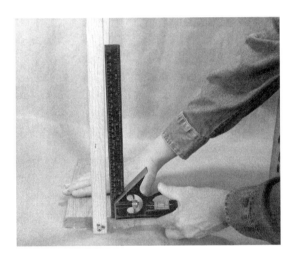

10. The strings are the next step in the assembly. Cut a piece of string that is approximately 5 inches longer than the length of the base. Tie a knot in one end and then lay it into one of the grooves cut into the top of the supports. Then bring the string over to the second support and insert it into this groove. Tie knots at a few different positions on the excess length of string from the second support; this will allow you to vary the tension on the string during experimentation.

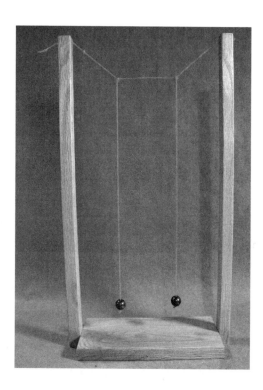
11. The pendulum strings can now be tied onto the support string. They should be the same length and about 3 to 4 inches apart on the support string. The knot attaching this string to the support string should allow it to slide to different locations for experimentation.

12. The last step in this assembly should be attaching the weights to the strings. For the best results, the length on each side should be the same.

13. Test the finished product by pulling one of the weights back slightly and releasing it. The first pendulum should swing shorter on each successive swing and the second pendulum should gain distance on each swing. After about 8 to 12 swings, the energy transfer should be complete. As the movement continues, the energy will start to transfer back to the first ball

Wood Model

Materials

- 1 block of wood, 1 × 6 × 12 in.

- 2 strips of wood, 1 × 1 × 36 in.

- 3 strips of wood, 1 × 1 × 14 in.

- 1 dowel rod, ½ in diameter × 6 in. long

- 2 dowel rods, ½ in. diameter × 1½ in. long

- 2 strips of wood ¼ in. thick × 2½ in. long

- 1 coiled spring toy

- 2 cube-shaped or wheel-shaped blocks of wood approximately 60 grams each

- 10 wood screws, 1½ in. long

- 4 wood screws, ½ in. long

For the wood frame, you can use 1 in. PVC piping and appropriate joints instead of the wooden pieces.

SAFETY NOTE

The following safety equipment is strongly suggested:

- Goggles for eye protection. NSTA recommends that you use safety goggles that conform to the ANSI Z87.1 standard and that provide both impact and chemical-splash protection for all science laboratory work.

- Dust mask to guard against breathing in airborne sawdust.

- Gloves whenever power tools are used.

Directions

1. Begin construction by cutting a dowel into a 6-inch length. The 2 thin strips of wood are measured against the coiled spring. Cut them approximately 1 inch longer than the outside diameter of the coil.

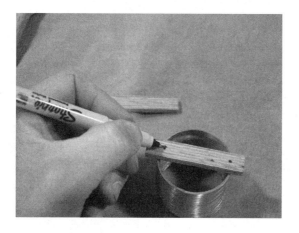

2. After you cut the thin strip of wood, center it on top of the coiled spring and mark 2 spots that are slightly inside of the inner diameter of the coil. Drill these marks to accept the ½-inch wood screw.

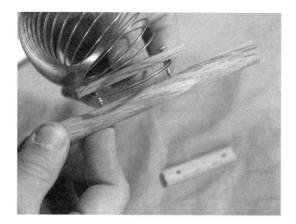

3. After drilling the holes, insert the screws into the short strip of wood. The screws should fit inside 2 turns of the end of the coil.

    Mark these positions of the screws on the wood dowel and drill pilot holes into the dowel.

4. If a sander is available, sand and flatten out the position where the spring sits on the dowel. This creates more contact area and gives a better hold on the string between the wooden dowel and the thin strip of wood that is screwed into it.

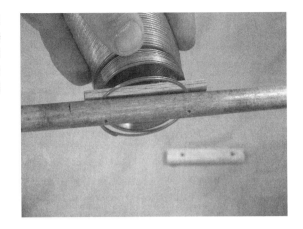

5. Use wooden blocks as the rotating masses on the dowel rod. The blocks can be 2-inch to 3-inch, cubic-shaped or wheel-shaped. The mass of each block should be the same, adjusted to about 60 to 70 grams.

6. Drill a ½-inch hole through the center of the block or wheel. This hole must allow a snug fit onto the ½-inch dowel. Friction must hold the blocks in place but still allow the blocks to be adjusted in and out for balancing with a bit of effort.

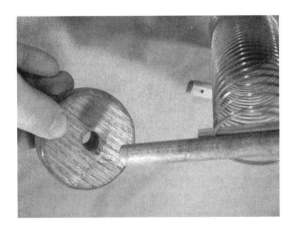

7. The completed pendulum mass is shown with the dowel and blocks in place. Because this assembly is hanging from a spring, the blocks will not be an equal distance away from the center of the dowel rod. One side must be adjusted in closer than the other to make the dowel level.

8. Before building the frame, you should test the action of the Wilberforce pendulum using a temporary upper support setup such as the one shown in the clay model instructions on p. 76.

This construction does not require using the whole spring. Several companies produce a suitable spring for this demonstration, but these springs may differ in strength and dimensions and could affect the results slightly. You should start with about 25 to 28 turns of the spring between the top and the bottom.

After trying the Wilberforce pendulum movement, you may have to make an adjustment in the height of the framing to compensate for longer spring movements.

9. The completed base assembly shows how the bottom section should be put together. The wood strips that the wood plate sits on are added for two reasons. They give the whole device more stability when it is in operation, and they help to anchor the tall vertical supports to the base.

10. The start of the base uses two of the wood strips screwed into what will be the underside of the base. It is important that the edges of the strip and the edge of the base plate are flush with each other.

11. Position the 3-foot vertical uprights flat against the table and then center them against the base. Two screw holes are needed. Fasten 1 screw into the bottom wood strip and the other into the wood plate.

12. Measure the top cross-support piece to the outside ends of the upright supports. Adjust the length of this bar to make the framing as squared as possible.

13. After cutting the cross member to length, drill a single pilot hole down through the 2 pieces of wood. Sink the screw into the framing to tie the pieces together.

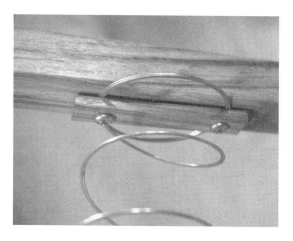

14. Several trials should help determine what length of spring gives the best results. Excess spring material can be cut off, since only 2 or 3 turns of the spring are needed for attachment. The attachment of the spring to the support bar resembles the attachment of the spring to the dowel at the bottom. Drill 2 holes into the small strip of wood, and then screw it into the underside of the support bar. Once again, the spring is held firmly between the 2 pieces of wood.

15. Drill two ½-inch holes into the upper side of the cross support. One hole is located on either side of the spring location. Glue the short dowel rods into these holes.

16. The purpose of these short dowels is to provide a convenient location for storing the wooden blocks.

17. For the initial trial of the pendulum, position the blocks toward the inside of the dowel. Make sure the dowel and blocks are hanging level. One block may have to be moved slightly closer to the center. Gradually fine-tune by moving the blocks out farther away from the spring until the pendulum demonstrates a complete change from a vertical to a tensional movement. The change from one type of oscillation to the other usually takes about 6 movements. You should see 1 or 2 complete vertical movements without any twisting of the block and dowel assembly. The change occurs over about 4 or 5 movements until only tensional oscillation is observed. This movement of twisting back and forth should last for 1 or 2 oscillations without any movement in the vertical direction. The pattern of changing from one type of motion to the other repeats itself until all of the energy dies out of the system. Once the location has been determined for the blocks, draw light pencil marks on the dowel for future reference.

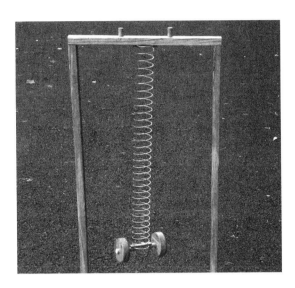

Clay Ball Model

Materials

1 wood dowel, ½-in. diameter × 6 in. long

1 clay ball, 120 to150 g

1 coiled spring toy

1 roll of duct tape

1 tongue depressor

1 meterstick

Directions

1. Use duct tape to attach the 6-inch dowel rod to the bottom of the coiled spring. The dowel rod should be centered to the middle of the spring.

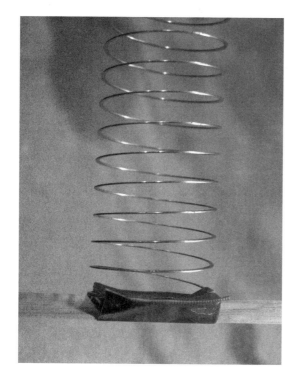

2. The clay masses need to be equal in size with an approximate mass of 60 to 65 grams each. Compare them on a trip balance to see that they have the same mass.

3. After making sure that the slabs of clay are equal, roll them into round balls. Each ball is pushed onto the dowel about halfway between the spring and the end of the dowel. The one side will need to be placed slightly closer to the spring to make the assembly hang level.

   Try holding the spring with about 25 turns in the spring section that can move. To get the pendulum to move correctly, there are two ways to adjust the movement: Change the amount of spring that you are holding or adjust the position of the clay balls on the dowel.

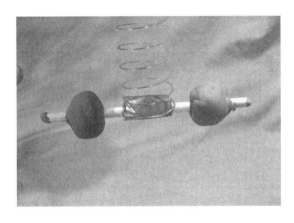

4. Determine the approximate length of the spring needed to show a complete change from the vertical movement to the torsional movement. Add 2 turns to the needed length and then cut off the excess spring.

5. Slide a piece of duct tape under the 2 turns of coil.

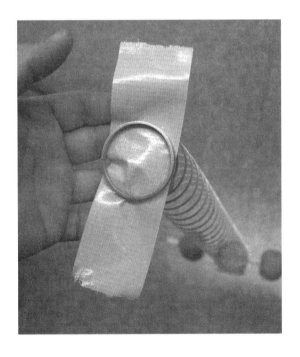

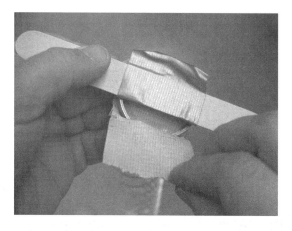

6. Attach the spring to a tongue depressor or similar wood strip using the duct tape.

   The tongue depressor makes it more convenient for setup and dismantling. It is easier to attach the tongue depressor to any convenient support rather than having to attach the spring directly with duct tape.

7. The picture shows the complete setup ready to go. When the tongue depressor is attached to a support rod, the spring will extend down about 18 inches.

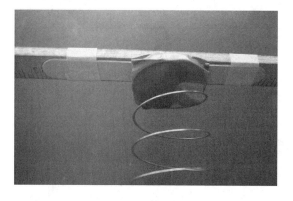

8. The tongue depressor is shown attached to the underside of a meterstick. It is held in place using masking tape or rubber bands. The meterstick can be supported between 2 ring stands, 2 backs of 2 student chairs, 2 desks, or any other convenient method of support.

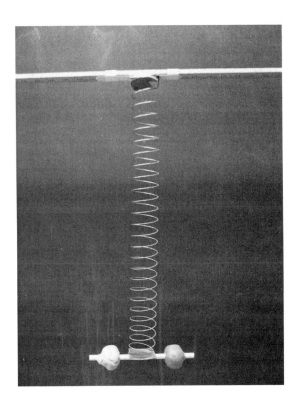

9. Put the clay balls near the spring for the initial trial of the pendulum. Make sure the dowel and balls are hanging level. One ball may need to be moved slightly closer to the center than the other side. Gradually fine-tune by moving the balls further away from the spring until the pendulum demonstrates a complete change from a vertical to a tensional movement. The change from one type of oscillation to the other usually takes about 6 movements. You should see 1 or 2 complete vertical movements without any twisting of the ball and dowel assembly. The change occurs over about 4 or 5 movements until only tensional oscillation is observed. This movement of twisting back and forth should last for 1 to 2 oscillations without any movement in the vertical direction. The pattern of changing from one type of motion to the other repeats itself until all of the energy dies out of the system. Once the location has been determined for the clay balls, draw light pencil marks on the dowel for future reference.

Instructional Information

Overview

Hero of Alexandria, in about 62 AD, demonstrated that a small amount of water could be lifted to a point higher than its origin. This apparently contradicts that water can rise only to its own level. But a few soda bottles, some tubing, and a few other simple materials can be assembled into a device that spurts a beautiful little fountain about a foot or two above its catch basin for 15 minutes or longer.

Student Skills

Observation. To understand the operation of the fountain, students must trace the complete movement of water from the upper bottle reservoir, through the tubing that forms the fountain, and then down through the hose to the lower bottle.

Application. Using a hose and a container of water, students can demonstrate the movement of water by producing their own simple siphon. They can also try other applications of this principle using other common materials to perform simple experiments.

Research. Students can research natural examples of intermittent fountains.
Communication. Students can demonstrate understanding by using the demonstrated process in re-writing the nursery rhyme "Jack and Jill."

Related Concepts or Processes

Intermittent fountains	Hydraulics
Siphons	Pneumatics
Potential energy	Pressure of gases
Kinetic energy	Pascal's principle
Pressure	

Prior Knowledge

Hero's fountain can be used with students from the elementary level through high school. Elementary students should have some understanding about gases. They should know that air is a gas and that it is made of small particles. They should further know that if we put the particles in a closed container, we can squeeze the container and move the particles closer, and the pressure will increase. Students should also know a little bit about forces and gravity. Gravity pulls matter downward. We can give objects energy by lifting them up against gravity. Students may also have had experience with siphons and should know that they can move water from a higher area to a lower area.

Predemonstration Discussion

You can use some simple items to review concepts before or during the Hero's fountain display.

You can set up a siphon with a plastic hose and two containers to hold water. Two large soda bottles work nicely. As water drains from one container into the other, the catching container can be raised or lowered to see how the separation affects the rate of flow. A clear plastic hose and colored water will give a better view of the siphoning movement.

You can discuss air pressure inside a sealed container by passing around a few soda bottles for students to examine. You might start the discussion by asking what is inside an empty soda bottle and what the effects of squeezing the bottle are.

Possible questions for discussion include the following:
- What is a siphon?
- Who has ever used a siphon? What for?
- Why do you think the draining end of the hose must be lower than the pool of water we are trying to drain?

- What would happen if we had the container of drained water at the same level as the body of water we are trying to empty?
- What is air made of?
- Is an empty soda bottle ever really empty?
- If we put the cap on an empty soda bottle, is there still air inside?
- What happens to the air pressure inside the bottle if we squeeze it?
- If we could make the bottle bigger, what would happen to the pressure if we could increase the volume inside the bottle?

Suggestions for Presentation

You can put the fountain together and set it up before class. After you review the applicable concepts, the fountain can be started by pouring water into the catch basin for the fountain. The catch basin needs to be filled at least halfway with water to give the system enough energy to activate the movement. A sufficient amount of water must flow through the hose down to the lower bottle to increase the air pressure inside the bottle. If all of the water drains from the fountain catch basin, the built-up pressure will be lost from the lower bottle.

After the initial discussion of the operation of the fountain, you can try some additional demonstrations. Increasing the distance between the upper and lower bottle will give the bottles more energy and make the fountain go higher. Conversely, a decrease in the distance between the two bottles will decrease the fountain height. Pull the fountain tube out of the stopper in the catch basin, and the water flow will be much faster than when it is in place.

When all of the water has left the upper bottle, the system can easily be reversed and tried again. Carefully remove the stoppers from each bottle and switch them around. If you don't keep some water in the lower bottle, it tends to fall over.

Interactive questions for discussion could include the following:
- How is it possible for water to be lifted to a point higher than its original height?
- How does the water get pushed up the tube?
- What would happen if the positions of the bottles were switched?
- How might this occur in nature as an intermittent spring?
- What happens if the stopper is removed from either of the bottles? Why?
- What are the effects of lifting the upper bottle higher?
- What are the effects of lowering the upper bottle?
- During the operation of the fountain, is there an increase of pressure or a decrease of pressure in the lower bottle?
- How does air pressure in the bottles compare?
- How can fluids be used to transfer pressure from one area to another?
- Why can fluids be used to transfer pressure from one area to another?

To clarify the process of how the fountain works, a few changes can be made to illustrate the operation.

Remove the stopper, catch basin, and small dropper tube. Attach the loose hose to the long plastic tube that delivered water to the fountain. Fill the upper bottle with water and move the catch bottle to a lower position. To start the siphon, pinch the air hose to keep the air from flowing from one bottle to the other. Next, squeeze the upper bottle until the water fills the siphon hose. Release the air hose and the siphon will start.

This setup acts like a typical siphon but occurs within a closed system. One hose moves the water; the other hose moves air to replace the water. Try disconnecting the hose that moves the air from bottle to bottle. The fountain will function as a siphon.

You could discuss the following questions:
- Does the siphon require both hoses to work?
- Is the air pressure in the lower bottle forcing the water to move?
- What would happen if the hose that is moving the air from bottle to bottle were disconnected?
- Will disconnecting the air hose have any affect on the amount of water moved?

After removing the hose that moved air from one bottle to the other, notice that the siphon still works.

Try sealing one of the open holes in either of the stoppers in the bottles. This can be done with a finger or by pushing something small into the hole. Clay works well. The water will soon stop flowing from the upper bottle to the lower bottle.

Why does the water stop flowing when the upper air hole is sealed? The water stops because an equal volume of air in the upper bottle cannot replace it. Pressure is decreased until no more water can leave the bottle.

Why does the water stop flowing when the lower air hole is sealed? The water stops because the water added to the bottle increases air pressure in the lower bottle. Eventually the pressure becomes equal to the force, pulling the water down, and the water stops moving.

Postdemonstration Activities and Discussion

- Have students measure the rate of water flow using a siphon. Have them devise a plan to see if the distance between the source and the release point makes a difference.
- Students can set up a table, collect data, and graph the results. A typical experiment might have 10 trials in which the bottles are lowered by 20-centimeter increments for each trial. The amount of water moved is measured for a 30-second or 1-minute period.
- Have students trace the operation of Hero's fountain and explain its operation.
- Research Hero of Alexandria. He is credited with several other inventions.
- How high can water be lifted using a siphon? (34 feet)
- Have students write a short story about how the nursery rhyme "Jack and Jill" could be rewritten by using their understanding of the concepts of siphons and potential energy. Why was it unnecessary for these two children to go up the hill for water?
- Cartesian divers are a very popular study activity for students of all ages. They can be as simple as using an eyedropper inside a soda bottle or can get a bit more involved.

Discussion of Results

Hero's fountain is a classic demonstration that uses the elastic properties of air to drive a small amount of water higher than its origin. As much as it might seem to be a perpetual machine, we are not getting something for nothing. Energy does have to be put into this system by lifting the mass of water and giving it potential energy. Although it is true that the fountain does lift water to a point higher than its origin, the end result is a net loss of energy. The water ends up at a point lower than where it started. This is the same action that occurs in the simple siphon. Water does go higher than its starting point but ends up lower than before. It is like a ball rolling down a hill: The end result is that matter ends up lower than where it started.

Pascal's principle—that pressure is always felt in all directions undiminished—can explain how pressure is affected within closed containers. The principle can apply to one single container or a series of containers connected with hoses. This means that the pressure in both bottles will start out equal and strive to remain balanced. If air pressure is increased in one bottle, it will be felt in the second bottle. The air hose connecting the two bottles will transmit higher pressure from one area to another. This is a principle of pneumatics.

To start the fountain, water is added to the upper catch basin. It then runs down the drain tube into the lower bottle. As the water enters the lower bottle, it compresses the air in the lower bottle. According to Pascal's principle, this increase in air pressure is transmitted via the plastic hose to the upper bottle. As more water drains down, the remaining air continues to be compressed. Eventually, as the air pressure becomes great enough, it will push some water up the tube to form the fountain.

When the water shoots up out of the little tube to form the fountain, it gets caught by the catch basin underneath. The water caught in the basin drains down through the tube and continues to compress air in the lower bottle.

Additional Activities

The following are a few additional projects that students can try that are instructive in the areas of energy, hydraulics, and pressure.

The Tantalus cup is an interesting device that can challenge students in their observations. The cup can be half filled with water and nothing will happen. After more water is added, the water will begin to drain out of the cup leaving it just about empty.

Cut the funneled section off a soda bottle to make the cup. Add an inverted stopper to the bottom.
Make the straw from rigid clear plastic tubing (available at most hardware stores). Heat it over a low burner and then bend it to form a question-mark shape. Add a bit of liquid soap to the plastic while inserting it into the stopper.

As the water fills the cup, nothing will happen until it is completely full. The tube fills with water and will then act as a siphon to drain the liquid.

Students can research the story of Tantalus and why this cup is named after him.

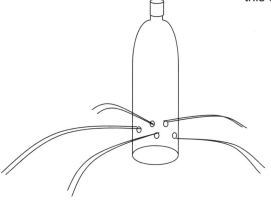

An additional demonstration of Pascal's Principle can be shown using a 20-ounce soda bottle. Drill five or six small holes into the sides of the bottle toward the bottom. The holes should be drilled rather than poked to ensure they are uniform in size and smooth on the edge. Then fill the bottle with water and seal it using the cap. Water will leak from the holes until the cap is on.

Squeeze the bottle and matching streams should come out of each hole drilled in the bottom. According to Pascal's principle the pressure is felt throughout the container and water is pushed out each hole evenly.

A commercially produced Hero's fountain called Fountain Connection is available in science catalogs. Each time the bottle is turned over; a spurting fountain is produced inside the bottle.

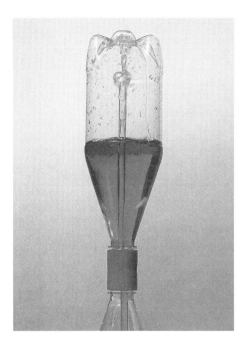

Directions for Assembly

Materials

2 2-liter soda bottles

1 3-liter soda bottle or a large plastic lid

2 2-holed rubber stoppers, size 3

1 2-holed rubber stopper, size 6

2 pieces of soft plastic hose, 3 ft. long

3 pieces of small diameter rigid plastic tubing, 4 in. long

2 pieces of small diameter rigid plastic tubing, 12–13 in. long

1 plastic or glass dropper

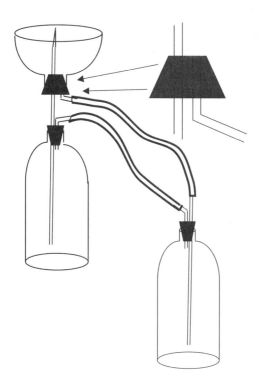

Enlarged view of rubber stopper.
The fountain tube is made from two separate pieces and is held together inside the stopper.

Drawing shows basic setup for bottles, tubes, hoses, and stoppers.

Directions

1. Remove the labels from all 3 soda bottles. The glue holding the labels on can be heated either with hot water, with a hair dryer, or by putting the bottle in a microwave for 15 seconds. You can remove remaining glue on the bottles by wiping it with an oil solvent or products such as WD-40.

SAFETY NOTE

Plastic tubing is preferable to glass. If you choose glass, additional safety precautions are needed to guard against burns or being cut from broken glass. NSTA recommends that you use fire-polished glass only and that you not use glass at all unless you have specific training.

The following safety equipment is strongly suggested:

- Goggles for eye protection. NSTA recommends that you use safety goggles that conform to the ANSI Z87.1 standard and that provide both impact and chemical-splash protection for all science laboratory work.

- Leather gloves for hand protection.

2. Use a heat source such as a stove or propane torch on low heat to warm the center of one of the 3 short plastic tubes. As the tube is heated gently, apply pressure to bend the tubing about 120 degrees. Repeat this step with a second short straw. The third short straw does not need to be bent.

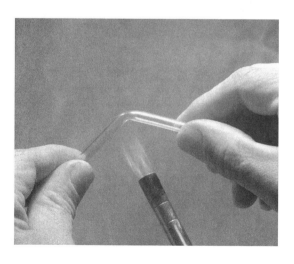

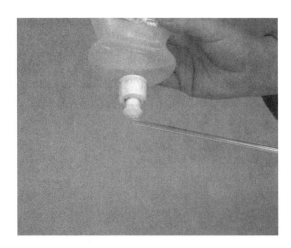

3. When assembling the rigid tubes into the stoppers, add a bit of dishwashing liquid to the tubes before insertion. Soap makes it easier to slide the tubing into the rubber stoppers.

SAFETY NOTE

If glass tubing is used, wear work gloves as a precaution in case it breaks. NSTA recommends that you use fire-polished glass only and that you not use glass at all unless you have specific training.

4. With a drop or two of liquid soap poured onto the end of each tube, gently twist the tubes while pushing the ends into the stoppers. This makes it easier to insert the tubing into the stoppers.

5. To make it easier to slide the soft plastic hose over the ends of the rigid plastic tubing, gently heat the hose over a low heat source such as a stove burner or a lit candle to soften the plastic and make it more pliable.

6. The upper tube assembly shown at the right should have the long tube supporting the larger inverted stopper by about 3 inches. This is just enough clearance for the 2 short plastic tubes. The long tube is inserted only halfway into the large inverted stopper. The inverted stopper will act as a connection between the long tube and the final fountain tube. The drawing at the right shows a close-up view of this connection.

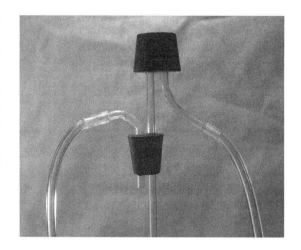

7. The lower tube assembly shown at the right shows this section fitted into the lower bottle. If there is not enough room to attach the hoses onto both tubes, the shorter tube can be bent as described in step 2.

   The height and duration of the water fountain is partly dependent on the size of the opening of the fountain tube tip that extends up from the large stopper. A small hole at the tip will give a fine stream of water that may last up to 20 minutes.

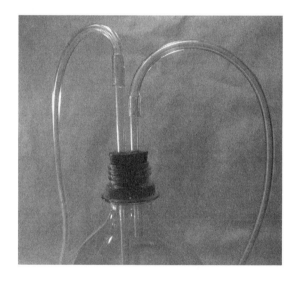

8. The final tube used for the fountain can be made from a few different sources. To make one out of glass tubing, heat a 12-inch length of glass tubing over a propane burner. When the glass is hot enough, it will glow a bright orange. With a gentle steady tug, it will pull like taffy. The glass will stretch and narrow into a fine thread. Break the thread off until a very fine hole is revealed.

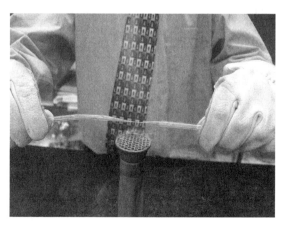

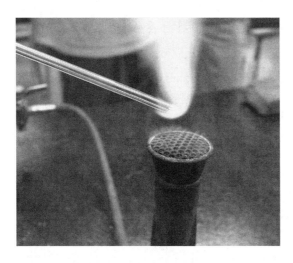

To fire polish the holes at both ends, hold the rough edge into the flame once more. The glass will glow orange and then smooth itself in the flame.

Take care while handling hot glass. Allow it to cool thoroughly before handling. Do not place hot glass in water or it will shatter.

This step has been somewhat successful with plastic tubing, but the results do not match the quality of glass.

9. The fountain tube must be handled with care; the point is still narrow and sharp. The tip is quite fragile and easily broken if dropped or handled roughly. It might be worthwhile making several tips as spares. The diameter of the tip can also be varied to experiment with the size and duration of the fountain.

    The glass stem on a medicine dropper may be used as the fountain tube.

10. You can make a fountain tube more safely and more easily from a disposable plastic dropper. Use scissors to cut the bulb from the plastic tube section.

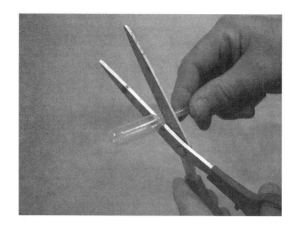

11. The narrow tip at the other end is usually too fine for a good stream. Cut the thin end off; more can be removed later if it is still too small.

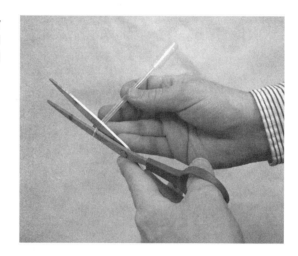

12. The next step is to insert the handmade glass or plastic fountain tube halfway down into the large inverted stopper. This tube should match up with the long tube that extends down into the soda bottle. Refer back to the setup diagram.

   It is important that the fountain tube fit tightly into the stopper. If it is loose, a few wraps of tape around the bottom of the tube can make it fit a bit tighter.

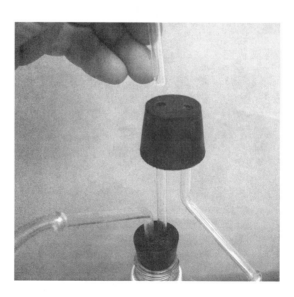

13. Use scissors to cut off the 3-liter soda bottle top. Cut the bottle about where the bottom cylinder starts to funnel into the top section. Invert the funneled end of the 3-liter bottle and slip it down onto the inverted large stopper; push firmly to ensure a good seal.

14. The 3-liter bottle top will catch most of the water from the fountain, but will still allow some to fall to the tabletop. The fountain tube can be twisted and angled slightly during operation to adjust the stream so that the inverted bottle top catches the bulk of the falling water.

15. You can make a larger catch basin from a large plastic lid. The one pictured was from a lettuce crisper container. Cut a 1-inch hole directly in the center of the lid. This can be done by placing the plastic lid on top of a piece of scrap wood and then using a wood bit on a slow drill speed. The smaller end of the stopper should be a tight fit into the hole made into the plastic lid.

16. During the final assembly, you must push the stoppers firmly into the bottle tops to ensure a good seal. Any leaks of air or water will defeat the operation of this device. The operation starts with filling the upper soda bottle ¾ full with water. If you use colored water, it will splash out of the catch basin and could stain nearby materials. The picture shown uses colored water only for better visibility. The bottom bottle needs a small amount of water to keep it from falling over. Pour water into the fountain catch basin and fill it about ½ full. Water will drain down into the lower bottle and start the fountain process.

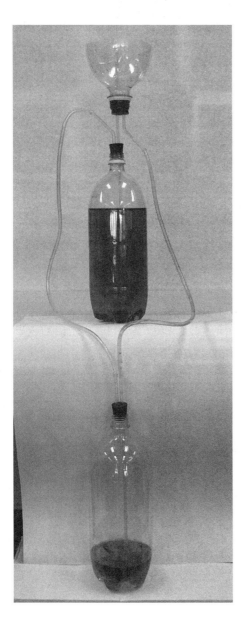

Instructional Information

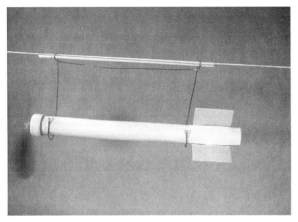
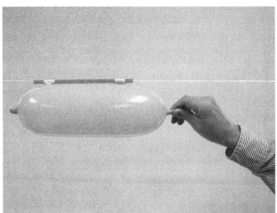

Overview

String racers are an effective way to demonstrate Newton's third law. This set of instructions gives plans for two types of string racers: the simple balloon racers that are quick and easy to build and a rubber band–powered propeller design that can race down a string 80 feet or more. Both of these pieces can be built and demonstrated simply as an example of action-reaction, or they can be incorporated in a project-building assignment for students to test a variety of design objectives.

Student Skills

Observation. The string racer and the balloon will move forward as a result of air pushed backward.

Design and Construct. Students can build a copy of the string racer with the plans provided, or they can design their own version and try to improve its performance. Other variations of the propeller and tube can be adapted for use on land or water.

Application. Students can look for other examples of propulsion or forward movement as a result of air being pushed backward.

SAFETY NOTE

The moving propeller can hurt fingers or cut skin if it hits someone while it is spinning. Students must be careful not to let the spinning propeller hit their fingers upon release and must not try to catch the racer before it stops.

The string racer can move quite quickly down the string, possibly jumping off the holder along the way. Instruct students to stand back from the moving string racers.

Related Concepts or Processes

Potential energy	Friction
Kinetic energy	Newton's second law
Inertia	Newton's third law
Simple machines	Speed
Design	Testing of hypothesis
Trial and error	Construction techniques

Prior Knowledge

You can use these pieces for early elementary students if you use them as a demonstration. Younger students should be able to define motion. It would be helpful if they have been introduced to the application of force as a push or a pull. They should understand that forces are needed to make things move and that friction will slow objects down and eventually stop them. Older students should have some basic understanding about motion and how we can measure it. They may have been introduced to some ideas about storing energy versus energy being used. These pieces also can be used to demonstrate Newton's laws of motion.

Predemonstration Discussion

Students can review the ideas of how forces are applied and energy is needed to make objects move through numerous examples. You should show wind-up toys, lifting a ball up and then allowing it to roll down a table, and the balloon racer before the string racer. A number of questions are applicable; use those that apply to the age of your students.

Some questions for discussion might include the following:
- What is needed to make an object move?
- How can we add energy to make things move?
- What are some ways that toys or objects can store energy?
- What are some ideas that affect the distance that an object will move?
- Why do moving objects slow down?

Suggestions for Presentation

Thread a long string through a drinking straw and then tie it so it extends from one end of the room to the other. A successful sequence might start with a demonstration of a deflated balloon and a discussion of how energy can be added to the balloon. After energy is added, students can discuss how the balloon will move if it is released. If you have other shapes of balloons, discuss what flight characteristic each might have.

The discussion about the untethered balloon should lead into attaching the balloon to the string. This will allow for a more efficient movement. The string will help to stabilize the movement of the balloon and will direct the air backward. The balloon is then propelled forward, usually at a higher rate of speed than in the untethered mode, because less energy is lost to extraneous movements.

The propeller-driven string racer can follow the balloon racer. Attach the wire holder to the string. It is easier to wind up this string racer first and then attach it to the holder. Try not to pull down on the string racer as the propeller is released, because that will make it bounce up and waste a lot of energy.

Interactive questions about balloon energy could include the following:
- Does a deflated balloon have any potential energy?
- How can we put energy into it?
- What happens if I let the inflated balloon go?
- Why does it not travel in a straight path?
- How can we get the balloon to travel in a straight path?

Interactive questions about the balloon racer could include the following:
- How does the flight characteristic change when the balloon is tethered to the string?
- Compare the speed of the tethered and the untethered balloons.
- Why does the tethered balloon move faster?
- If the balloon goes forward, what must the particles of air do?
- How would the amount of air put into the balloon affect the speed and distance that it travels?
- How can we calculate the speed of this racer?

Interactive questions about the propeller-driven racer could include the following:
- What are the similarities between the balloon racer and the propeller racer?
- What are the differences between the balloon racer and the propeller racer?
- How does this vehicle move?
- How does a propeller push air backward?
- What are some variables that might change the speed and distance that the racer travels?
- How can we calculate the speed of this vehicle?

Postdemonstration Activities and Discussion

The propeller-driven string racer was originally designed as a building project for elementary students. A pattern was printed on heavy stock paper by using a copying machine. The bottle caps had holes added to them, and students would assemble the propeller system. It is a simple project that fourth- and fifth-graders can build with some assistance from an adult. When used as a demonstration for middle school students, this propeller-driven racer generated the same enthusiasm it did in the younger children. Using the fact that the purpose of the fins is to keep the string racer from turning as it travels from one end to the other, middle school students found it interesting to use larger fins and adjust them so that the string racer would do two or three loops as it traveled from one end to the other.

Propeller-driven string racers can also be the basis for a design project. Give students a variety of materials, and challenge them to construct a device that will travel down the string as quickly as possible. You can show the string racer as an example of how it can be done, although this usually results in students' copying it and may limit the designs students will try.

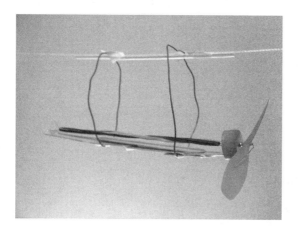

The picture is a typical example of a student-designed string racer. In this case, students were not shown any examples before they were given the assignment.

Students tried using the propellers to push or pull the string racer. Both ways can be successful. Most students stick with a single propeller, some tried using 2 propellers and a few tried 3. Usually, the simplest designs are the most effective.

Suggested materials

Purchased propellers or propellers made from tongue depressors, soda bottle caps, soda bottles, cardboard, paper, mat board, 18-gauge steel wire, foam meat trays, paper clips, 8-inch-long rubber bands, balsa wood, glue gun, tape, wheels, K'nex, Lego's.

The string racers can demonstrate several concepts of force and motion. For example, they show potential energy changing into kinetic energy. The balloon racer stores energy (potential) by stretching the latex fabric. This energy changes into kinetic energy by pushing the gases out of the end. The string racer stores energy by twisting the rubber band and uses the propeller to pull the device through the air as it pushes air backward.

String racers can demonstrate Newton's laws of motion. The devices will continue traveling forward even after the balloon empties or the rubber band unwinds. This is an example of inertia. Both of these pieces slow down and eventually stop due to friction between the string and the straw. Newton's second law explains the relationship between force, mass, and acceleration. The movement of the racers can demonstrate how an increase of mass can decrease the acceleration. You can also demonstrate Newton's second law by changing the force. The amount of force is determined by how many rubber bands are turning the propeller, so changing the number of rubber bands will affect the acceleration. Newton's third law talks about action and reaction. Both of these devices go forward by applying a force backward. In either case, students can feel the air particles being moved backward.

Additional Activities

Have students keep a journal to trace their progress through this problem-solving activity. Design sketches can be part of the journal, and they should include ideas that worked and those that did not.

Another form of transportation for the propeller-powered tube can be some type of wheeled car. The base supports are carved out of foam insulation material. The wheel and axles fit through a plastic drinking straw. The straw is glued into place using a hot glue gun. Rubber bands are used to attach the propeller tube to the supports.

> **SAFETY NOTE**
>
> The moving propeller can hurt fingers or cut skin if it hits someone while it is spinning. Students need to be careful not to let the spinning propeller hit their fingers or skin.

Directions for Assembly

Propellers

Materials

- 2 sheets of heavy stock paper
- 1 soda bottle cap, any size
- 2 small paper clips
- 1 small plastic bead
- 1 plastic drinking straw
- 3 rubber bands
- 16–20 in. of thin gauge wire
- 1 plastic propeller or tongue depressor for home-made propeller
- plastic or masking tape
- 50-plus ft. of string

The string racer and variations are all based on the same design using the tube and propeller as the power supply source.

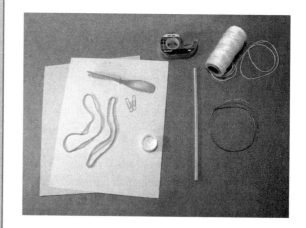

Directions

1. To make the tube for the body, start by cutting the three slits into the bottom corner of the heavy stock paper. The slits are needed for the fins of the tail section to fit through.

   Cut the slits 2 inches long and 1 inch apart.

   Start them ½ inch from the right side edge and ½ inch from the bottom edge. Use a pen to draw thick lines onto the stock paper.

2. You can cut the slits using the edge of the scissors as a cutting edge.

3. After cutting the slits for the fins, roll the paper into a cylinder shape a few times to help retain this shape. Use a large dowel rod as a guide for the rolling process. Make sure the slits appear on the outermost layer of this tube instead of on the inside.

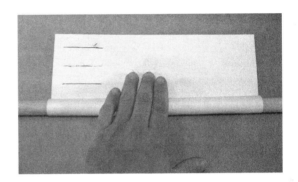

4. The tube will eventually fit snuggly in a soda bottle cap. Use the bottle cap to determine the correct size.

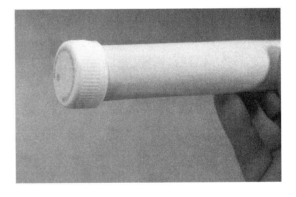

5. Make the fins for the tail section from another piece of heavy stock paper. Use a ruler to measure and then draw a pattern that is 2 inches wide and 10 inches long. Use a ruler to measure and then mark off 1-inch blocks for the folding lines. Draw 9 lines across the 2-inch width of the tail section.

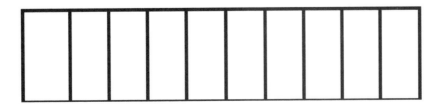

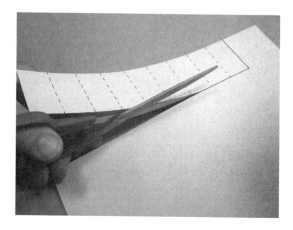

6. Cut out the 2-inch × 10-inch section with scissors.

7. The pattern for folding the tail section is below. Each line indicates where to fold the heavy stock paper.

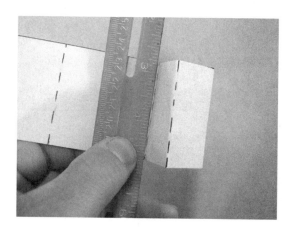

8. Use a straight edge in the folding process to help ensure the folded lines match the drawn lines. The folds must be accurate to ensure that they match up with the slits cut in the body tube.

9. The creases in the paper must be well defined. Lay the fold on a hard surface and press and slide the ruler against the fold. Do this with each fold.

10. Fold the tailpieces tightly together. Each tail fin is made from two pieces of the paper folded together. You can cut these fins to resemble a rocket-tail assembly after they are inserted in the tube body.

11. Unroll enough of the body tube so that the folded tabs for the tail section can be inserted into the slots cut into the body tube.

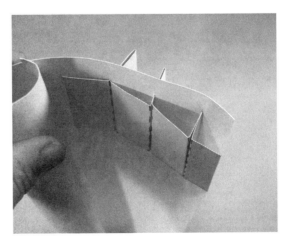

12. Roll the paper and fins back into the cylinder shape again. The fins should be evenly spaced in the back end of the cylinder.

    The fins help stabilize the string racer as it moves on the string. They can be adjusted to make the string racer do loops as it travels down the string.

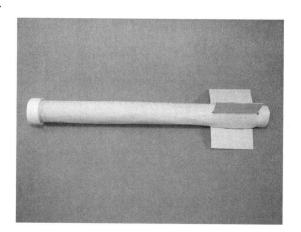

13. The tube diameter should be approximately the same as the inside diameter of the bottle cap. Check the tube diameter at the front and back end of the tube using the bottle cap.

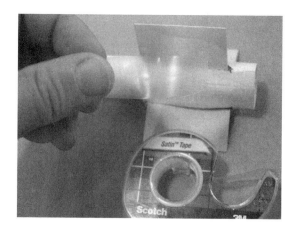

14. Apply a few pieces of tape in the tail section area and along the tube body to keep the tube from unrolling.

15. To make the propeller assembly, start by removing the inner liner from a soda bottle cap and then use a pointed object such as an ice pick or compass to poke a hole through the center. The hole should be just slightly larger than the diameter of the paper clip.

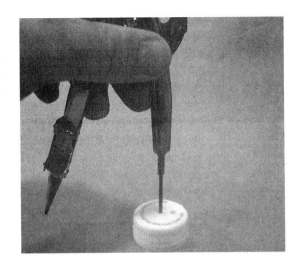

16. Make the shaft for the propeller from a paper clip. Unbend 2 of the 3 bends. Leave the smallest of the 3 bends in place. This shaft should resemble a "J." If the paper clip is too long, cut it using the cutting edge of pliers.

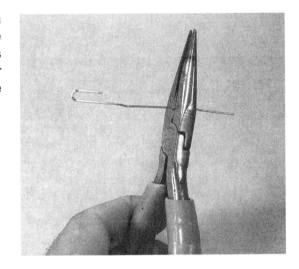

17. For a smoother operation, the propeller should turn in a straight path without any wobbles. The area where the shaft goes through the propeller is rounded. Sand the rounded tip of the propeller shaft flat, using a fine grit sandpaper or nail file.

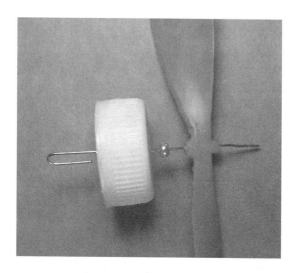

18. Begin the assembly of the propeller by pushing the straightened end of the paper clip through the hole in the soda cap. The hooked end of the paper clip is toward the inside of the bottle cap. Now add a small bead with flat ends to the paper clip shaft, followed by the propeller. The bead will act as a washer between the cap and propeller and allow it to turn more efficiently.

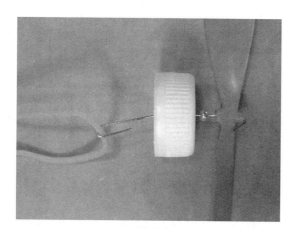

19. Use the pliers to bend over ¼ inch of the paper clip to catch the propeller.

The speed of the racer is dependent on the number of rubber bands used to propel it; 3 or 4 usually work very nicely. Hook the rubber bands onto the "J" portion of the paper-clip shaft. Bend the end of the paper clip over the rubber bands to hold them in place.

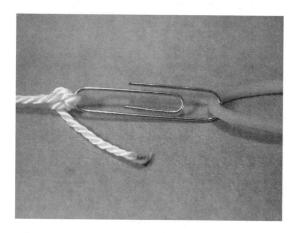

20. Hook the other end of the rubber band onto another paper clip. Tie a short string onto this paper clip to ease the fitting of the rubber bands through the body tube.

21. To assemble the propeller onto the body, hold the tube vertically and dangle the string into the tube. After the string comes through the opposite end of the racer body, pull on the string to stretch the rubber bands.

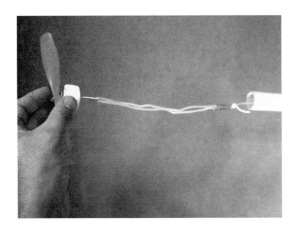

22. To attach the rubber bands to the racer body, hook one of the bends of the paper clip onto the tail section of the tube body.

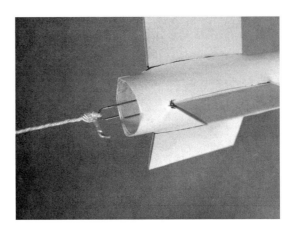

23. The body of the racer is completed. Wind it up and test it a few times to see how it spins. The propeller should spin without wobbling. If the propeller wobbles, then the paper clip shaft needs some minor adjustments. Do not overwind the rubber bands, or they will break inside the tube.

The final assembly of the string racer requires that the body be attached to a string that is tied across the room.

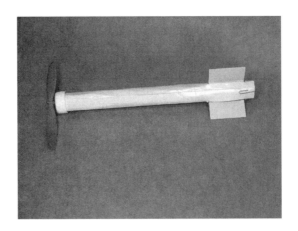

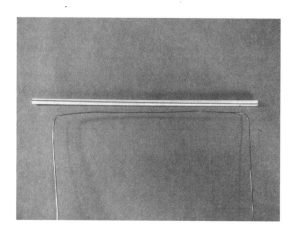

24. A simple method for attaching the racer to the string uses a drinking straw and 24 inches of metal wire. The wire can be bent to hold the racer body to the straw and allow easy attachment or removal of the racer for winding or repairs.

    Start by threading the string through the straw and then tie the string onto two supports.

    Measure and cut off about 24 inches of the wire. The middle 8 inches of the wire remains straight against the straw. Bend the outer sections 90 degrees to form a large "U" section.

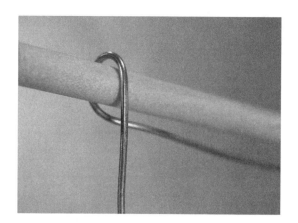

25. Bend over the top ½ inch of the 8-inch wire section to clip onto the straw. Use a dowel rod or pencil to form the bend in each corner of the wire. Don't make the bends too tight, or they will pinch the string inside the straw when it is attached.

26. Make the second set of bends in the wire hanger about 6 inches down from the straw. Wrap a 1-inch circular bend in the wire around the racer body to hold it in place. The bends must hold the racer enough beneath the straw so that the propeller does not come in contact with the string. Wrap the wire around the racer body for about ¾ of the distance around. Cut off the excess wire using wire-cutting pliers. The last ¼ inch of the wire should be folded back on itself to form a very small loop that makes a blunt edge.

27. The racer body is now ready for a practice run. Wind the rubber bands up by turning the propeller. Place the racer back onto the wire supports while holding the propeller and then let it go.

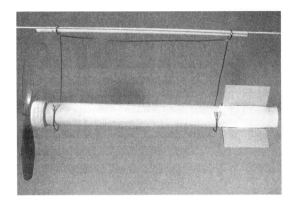

Alternate propellers

An alternative to purchased propellers is having students make their own. Several designs can be built and tested. Typical purchased propellers have the blades offset by 90 degrees.

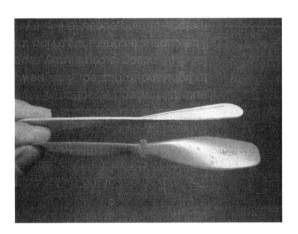

Directions

1. A tongue depressor can be formed into the same shape as a purchased propeller by twisting it 90 degrees from one end to the other.

2. If you soak the tongue depressor in water for about an hour, it will become soft and pliable and can be easily bent. A simple form for holding the tongue depressors has 4 horizontal and 4 vertical slits about 4 inches apart. Place the wet tongue depressors in this form until they dry. After they dry, they will retain the 90-degree twist. Then drill a hole in the center for the propeller axle.

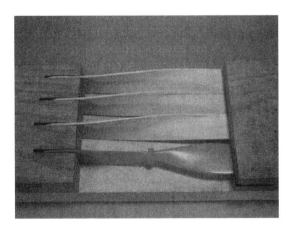

Section 6

Balloon Racers

Materials

- 1 straw
- 1 long thin balloon
- plastic tape
- 50-plus ft. of string

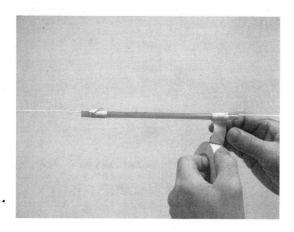

Directions

1. Thread a string through a drinking straw and tie it to 2 supports about 20 to 40 feet apart.

   Wrap a short piece of masking tape with the sticky side out on the front edge of the straw. Wrap another piece of tape with the sticky side out on the other end of the straw.

   Do not wrap the tapes too tightly around the straw. Success depends on whether the tape can slide back and forth on the straw with very little effort.

2. To operate this racer, blow up the balloon to its maximum size. While holding the balloon, lift it to the straw and press the center of the balloon onto the sticky sides of the tape.

    Release the balloon when you are ready. The balloon should race down the length of the string.

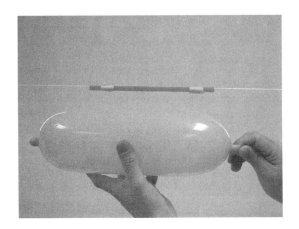

3. A successful trial should have the balloon still on the straw with both tapes moving toward the center of the straw.

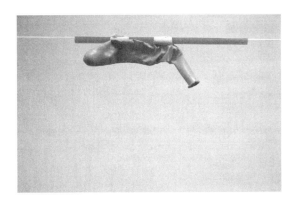

Instructional Information

Overview

Placed in bright sunlight or under a 100-watt bulb, this motor will spin up to 65 RPMs. The black ribs stretched across the cups are made from ordinary plastic bags. The polyethylene polymer strips of plastic contract as they are heated. This action changes the center of gravity of the rotor, and the assembly becomes unbalanced and starts to turn, exposing other ribs that continue the process.

Student Skills

Observation. Students will observe that the movement of the motor is dependent on full light or sunlight directed onto the solar wheel. Students can also stretch a piece of the plastic and then hold it near some heat. They will observe that the plastic shrinks as it is warmed.

Measurement. Students can make measurements of the work done by the motor and then determine the minimal amount of power exerted.

Trial and Error. Students can build their own motors and test methods to make the motor more efficient.

Research. Students can investigate methods of converting sunlight into other forms of energy.

Application. Students can look for other methods of turning sunlight into energy.

Related Concepts or Processes

Expansion of matter   Solar energy
Polymers   Center of gravity

Prior Knowledge

This piece of equipment can interest students at all levels.

The solar motor is an excellent way of demonstrating one method of changing solar energy directly into motion. For students to understand its operation, however, they need to understand some basic concepts. One is that matter can contract or expand due to temperature changes. Most materials expand as they are heated and then contract as they are cooled. Some substances do not follow this principle—plastics, for example. Another concept is that light is a form of energy. For energy to perform work, it must be changed from one type into another. A third concept that students need to know is that gravity is a force that pulls on all objects.

Predemonstration Discussion

This motor is useful for demonstration in several areas of science. It can be introduced in the study of methods of technology, and it can be used in chemistry in the study of polymers. It can be used in physics for the study of mechanics. It can also be used in lessons that review alternative energies. The limitations of energy supplies, the increasing demand for energy, and the need for cleaner energy production are additional topics to which this piece is relevant. Most students have probably seen examples of devices that convert sunlight into mechanical energy: You can present radioscopes, Stirling engines, and solar cells as examples of devices that do so. Some general questions that can be discussed before demonstrating this solar motor might include:
- What are some different types of energy?
- What is radiant energy?
- What colors are the most efficient at converting light into thermal energy?
- What is meant by alternative energy?
- How can we change sunlight into other forms of energy?
- What are some ways that solar energy can be incorporated in people's homes?
- What is passive solar energy?
- Where does most of the country's energy come from?

Suggestions for Presentation

This piece works well in direct full sunlight indoors, and it can be used outdoors on calm days. It can be used in summer or winter and will operate for most of the day.

If sunlight is not available, you can use a lamp with a 100-watt bulb if you are careful not to get it too close to the plastic strips. Before the solar motor is put into direct light, check to make sure the cup assembly is finely balanced. This will ensure that it operates properly. As the motor is put under an electric light source, it might be helpful to give it a gentle push to get it started and to keep the plastic from being heated too much so that it melts.

To explain the operation, start by taking a short strip of the plastic material and stretch it. Pass around additional samples for students to try. You can add a discussion of polymers at this time. Students can also discuss how most materials expand when heated. If the long piece of the stretched polymer is held under a 100-watt lightbulb and brought near the bulb, the plastic can be observed contracting. The next step in the explanation is to observe what happens to the cup assembly when it becomes top-heavy. To do so, tape a paper clip to the top of the assembly to demonstrate that the heavier side of the cup rotor will rotate to the bottom. You can ask students about what the strips will do to the cup assembly as the strips are exposed to light.

Some other questions you can ask of students include the following:
- Why are the ribs black?
- What happens to this plastic when it is gently heated?
- What do you think might happen if this material is cooled?
- Would this device work if a clear plastic were used instead of a black color?
- What happens to the cup assembly if it becomes top-heavy?
- What force causes the cup assembly to rotate?
- What changes might we try to make this motor spin faster?

Postdemonstration Activities and Discussion

- As a writing assignment, have students explain the process of how the motor operates.
- Students can do additional research on the characteristics of polymers.
- Students can research other methods of converting solar energy into other useful forms.
- A design problem might include designing other uses for the contracting ability of the polymer.
- Students can try building their own model and can then test variables such as additional mass on the flywheel and changes in the size and types of cups.
- The strips can be tested and altered by changing the color, the brand type, the thickness, the width, and the number.
- You can use mirrors to direct more sunlight onto the top strips; this additional energy can increase the performance. Using this method, the motors can reach speeds up to about 86 RPMs.

Discussion of Results

The movement of this motor is dependent on the unique property of the stretched trash bag strips, which are made from a plastic material called polyethylene. This chemical is a common example of a polymer. One of its characteristics is that it is made of very long molecular chains. These long molecules are stretched to their elastic limit during the stretching process. If more pressure is applied, these long chains are broken when the plastic tears apart. By heating the strips, the polymer chains contract, pulling the molecules closer together. They do not expand due to cooling as some students may suggest. The action of the polyethylene contracting is quite different from a uniform expansion of matter as a result of kinetic energy. As this plastic is heated temporarily, the material pulls tighter and shrinks to a smaller size. The plastic remains "shrunken" until pressure is applied to stretch the molecular chains out again.

The movement of the motor happens because the materials at the top of the cup assembly contract slightly; this action is pulling the cups together at the top. The action is not noticeable because it is so slight. It is noticeable if the plastic is heated sufficiently, but do not try it with the cup assembly. With the cups pulled together, the assembly becomes unbalanced. The motor is now top-heavy and starts to turn and fall toward the bottom. As the assembly turns, a new section is then exposed to light and is heated. This new spot becomes top-heavy, causing this section to fall. The action is continually repeated, making the top section always unbalanced. The cups are constantly trying to adjust to become balanced. The end result is the motor's turning because it is trying to right itself. The highest speed for the cups in direct summer sunlight seems to top out around 65 RPMs.

The addition of mass to the flywheel as suggested at the end of the assembly directions has some benefits and drawbacks. This addition can make the cup more efficient, but it will not make it spin faster. The good news is that it can enable this tiny motor to perform small tasks; the bad news is that the motor becomes more finicky and will require more adjustments for balancing.

Additional Activities

After you have mastered the basic assembly and operation of the solar motor, it may be time to put this motor to some useful tasks. The first project to tackle could be calculating the horsepower that one of these minidynamos is putting out.

To calculate power, you must make some adjustment to the design of the solar motor. The first change could be to replace the drinking straw support posts with something sturdier. A wooden dowel with nylon screws is an excellent choice for replacing the straw supports.

You will need to add mass to the flywheel to make it more efficient.

The cup lid on the opposite side should be changed; instead of cutting out a large hole in the lid, reduce it to a ¼-inch hole, the same diameter as the axle. This will direct all forces to the heavy flywheel.

The next change would be to extend the shaft by about two inches on one of the sides.

A very small hole is drilled into the wood shaft and then a half-inch hole is drilled directly below it into the base.

Tie a meter-long string onto the motor shaft and thread it down though the base hole. Extend the motor base over the side of a table; this is to allow the string to hang unobstructed.

The calculations of power require that the motor do some work. In this case, the motor is lifting 2 or 3 paper clips. The formula for work is force x distance (newtons x meters). Measure the mass of the paper clips in grams and convert to newtons. Measure how high the paper clips will be lifted; ½ meter is a suitable distance. Multiply the weight times the distance to get the work done in joules.

Calculate power by dividing the time in seconds into the work done (seconds into joules). Use a stopwatch to time how long it takes the motor to lift the paper clips. The calculations will yield the power in watts. It will be a very small amount.

Students will find it interesting to calculate the horsepower. One horsepower is equal to 746 watts. To calculate the horsepower, divide the number of watts by 746.

A reasonable number is about 1.5 millionths of a horsepower, or this can be expressed as 1.5 microhorsepower.

Sunshine Alarm

A design challenge for advanced studies can be to have students come up with ideas and then build attachments that can harness the microhorsepower of the solar motor.

In this example, a small flexible plastic arm has been added to the shaft (axle) of the motor. This little arm was cut from a cup's plastic lid. A nut is glued to the end of this plastic arm.

A wood support has been added to the end of the base. It has a small bell suspended from a cross arm. As the motor turns, the nut on the plastic spoke will hit the bell, telling you the Sun is shining.

The position of the bell can be adjusted by twisting the support, raising or lowering the bell, or by sliding the string across the bar.

Directions for Assembly

Materials

- 2 16-oz. plastic cups with lids
- 1 piece of rigid foam insulation, ½ in. to ¾ in. thick
- 1 black thin plastic trash bag
- 1 ¼-in. wood dowel, 11 in. long
- 1 wood block for base, 3 × 13 in.
- 1 piece aluminum metal tape
- 2 ¼-in. nylon washers
- 1 ¼-in. push nuts
- $^5/_{16}$-in. clear plastic tubes or drinking straws, 4 in. long
- 2 large straight pins

Directions

1. Start by cutting and sanding the wood for the base. Drill holes about ½-inch deep for the straws to fit into. They should be spaced about 11¼ inches apart. Put the straws into these holes, and then hold the wood dowel between the two supports to check the size. The dowel should fit loosely between the 2 straws. If the dowel is a tight fit, remove a small piece from one end of the dowel. The straws have small notches cut into them to hold the pin axle assembly. These are cut into the straw using a nail file like a small saw.

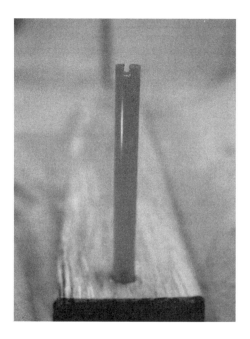

Solar Motor

SAFETY NOTE

The following safety equipment is strongly suggested:

- Goggles for eye protection. NSTA recommends that you use safety goggles that conform to the ANSI Z87.1 standard and that provide both impact and chemical-splash protection for all science laboratory work.
- Dust mask to guard against breathing in airborne sawdust.
- Gloves whenever power tools are used.

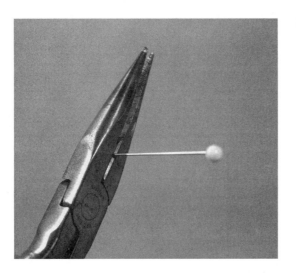

2. The pin axles will extend out from the dowel rod and rest in the straw supports. Both ends of the dowel must be drilled with holes before inserting the pin axles into them. Without pilot holes, the pins tend to bend when trying to insert them into the dowels. Cutting off the ends of a straight pin can make a homemade drill bit. Wrap a bit of tape around one end so that it will fit tightly into the drill chuck. With the pin in the drill chuck, cut the point off of the pin. This cut edge will act like a regular drill bit.

3. Do not attempt to drill holes into the dowel while holding it in your hand. The dowel can be clamped into a vise to hold it steady. Another method for holding the dowel during the drilling process can be made by drilling a ¼-inch hole into a scrap piece of wood. Insert the dowel into the hole, with the end of the dowel flush with the surface. Both ends of the dowel rod must be drilled with the homemade drill bit.

4. Before the cups can be mounted onto the dowel rod, you must make a ¼-inch hole in the center of the cup bottom. Do not use a drill bit because it may end up tearing up the bottom of the cup, making the holes too large and useless. The best method is to melt a hole through the cup by heating the nail or screwdriver just hot enough to push it through the plastic material. Before starting the hole, locate the center of the bottom and then trace a pattern using the end of the dowel rod as a guide.

5. The construction of the cup assembly starts with the first slide nut and nylon washer forced onto the wooden dowel. It will take some effort to get the slide nut onto the dowel. The nuts may bend slightly as they are wrestled onto the dowel. This is normal and will not hurt their integrity.

6. The position of the washer and slide nut can be determined by holding the dowel next to one of the cups. The dowel rod should extend past the mouth of the cup by about ½ inch. If the slide nuts have been pushed too far on the dowel rods, remove them by sliding them all the way off the dowel and start again.

7. For this motor to operate properly, the bottoms of both cups must be separated by at least ¼ to ½ inch during the motion of the motor. The spacer that will sit between the cup bottoms is cut out from the piece of Styrofoam insulation material. The diameter of the circle is 1 inch, and the hole in the center is ¼ inch in diameter. This spacer was made out of a scrap of foam insulation material and was cut out with a sharp knife blade used in a sawing motion. The spacer is ½ to 1 inch thick.

8. With the first cup in place on the dowel rod, the next step is to slide the foam spacer onto the rod and then follow it with the second cup. With both cups in the correct position on the dowel rods, the rods should extend out of the cups by an equal amount, preferably about ½ inch. If the ends of the rods do not extend out the same length, take the cups off of the dowel rod and adjust the position of the first slide nut. Since the nut slides only in one direction, you may have to slide it off the dowel and start over.

9. Once the cups have been adjusted to the correct position, it is now time to permanently attach the second washer and nut. Slide the second washer onto the dowel followed by the nut into the second cup. Once this second nut is slid onto the dowel rod, you will not be able to remove it. The whole cup assembly needs to be tightly held together. This requires that the second slide nut be pushed firmly down against the bottom of the second cup. A $^5/_{16}$-inch plastic or metal tube can be used to do this.

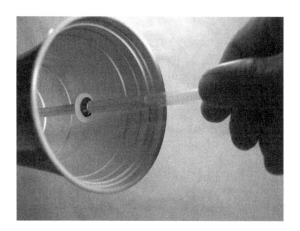

10. If a tube is not available, an alternative method is to position 6 pencils around the dowel and then wrap a rubber band around them to hold them in place. This can be used to push the slide nut down tight against the bottom of the cup.

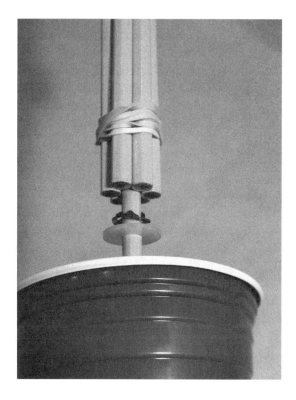

11. When you push the slide nut into position, it is helpful to position one end of the dowel down against the table. Push firmly with the tube or pencil assembly to make the slide nuts tight against the cup bottom. Turn the whole cup and shaft assembly over, and try this procedure from the opposite side.

12. The washers and nuts must be seated firmly against the bottom of each cup. The dowel rods must extend outside of the lip of the cup by at least ½ inch.

13. The dowel rods are now ready to have the pins inserted as the final portion of the axle. Try pushing the first pin into one of the ends of the dowel rod. It may be difficult to push the pins into the ends of the dowels more than ½ inch. The pins used as the axles may have to be shortened depending on their length. Use the cutting edge of the pliers to clip off the extra section of pin. With the pin axles in place, the assembly can be placed onto the base. The cup assembly should turn freely and should not rub against the straw supports. If the dowel rubs against the straws, take out one of the pin axles and sand or cut off a small section of the dowel rod and try it again.

14. It is now time to make the plastic strips that are responsible for the action of the motor. Cut the ribs from a thin black plastic garbage bag. The cheapest bags quite often are the best. The strips are 1½ inches wide and are cut parallel to the top of the bag. The length should be about 4 inches. Cut about 20 strips, as a few extra will be needed for practice. The edges must be cut smoothly with no jagged edges, or these will cause the plastic to tear during the next procedure.

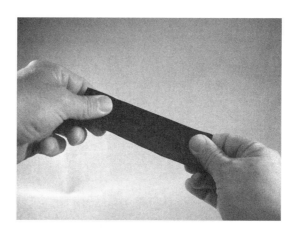

15. Stretching the plastic can be quite entertaining. This plastic material is a polyethylene polymer and must be stretched to near its breaking point. To stretch the plastic to the required thinness, grasp each end of the strip with a thumb and finger and pull very slowly and very firmly. It feels almost like stretching taffy or chewing gum. As the plastic is pulled, it will become much thinner and longer and will stretch out about 4 to 5 times its original length. The plastic will let you know when it has reached its elastic limit by breaking if it is pulled too far.

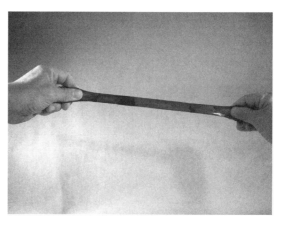

If You Build It, They Will Learn

16. You will use two methods to fasten the ribs permanently to each of the cups. The first is to use a 1-inch piece of plastic tape to attach the cut end of the plastic strip to the inside of a cup. About 1 inch of the strip should be taped inside the first cup.

17. Determine the length of the strip by stretching it to the inside of the second cup. Pull it gently to the inside of this second cup, and cut the strip long enough to have a 1-inch overlap inside the cup. Use the plastic tape to attach the strip to the inside of the second cup. It should be firm, but not too tight. These strips will adjust themselves to the right tension when they are heated.

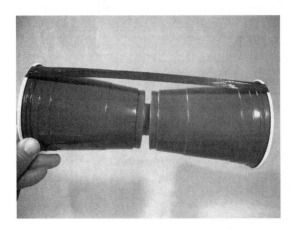

18. When the first strip is attached to both cups, it should bend the cups slightly toward each other on one side more than the other. Repeat the steps for stretching the rest of the plastic strips to get them ready for attaching to the cups. Place strip number 2 directly on the opposite side from strip number 1. Strip number 2 should be stretched tight enough to center and align the cups once again.

19. The third and then fourth strips should be added to the cup assembly an equal distance between the first 2 strips. These first 4 strips should be evenly spaced around the cups.

20. Put the assembly on the stand. The cups should be approximately centered and balanced on the dowel. Turn the cup assembly a half-turn and let it go. If the assembly is unbalanced, the heavy side will rotate to the bottom. To balance the cups, remove the tape from one end of the strip at the top of the cup assembly. Reapply the strip and tape again, but slightly looser to balance the cups.

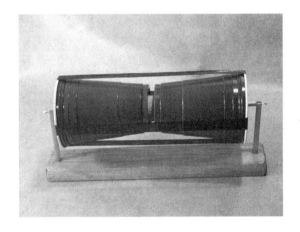

21. The drawing at the right shows the suggested order for applying the strips to the cup assembly. The sequence will help to ensure that the cups are approximately balanced during the assembly.

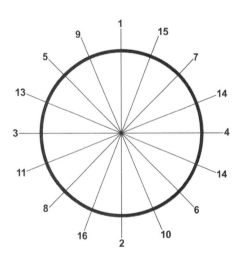

22. After completing the 8 strips, place the assembly back on its stand again to see that it is balanced. If the assembly appears to be unbalanced, loosen the strips toward the topside of the assembly and then reattach them. Complete the rotor by attaching the remaining 8 strips to the cup assembly. After they are added, check the balance and make any final adjustments if needed. It is difficult to get the assembly perfectly balanced. As part of the last step, an application of counterweights will fine-tune the balance of the assembly (step 25).

23. The second method of securing the strips onto the cups is attaching the plastic lids over the cups and strips. Use scissors to cut out most of the center portion of each cup lid. Leave the outer inch of the cup intact.

24. The lid can now be pressed onto the cup mouth and over the 16 strips. The lid will help lock the strips in place in case the tape fails to hold.

25. It is very important to the operation of the motor to have the cup assembly finely balanced. To do so, place the assembly back on the stand once again. If the assembly is unbalanced, the heavier side will rotate to the bottom. To balance out the assembly, the portion of the cups facing up needs to be made heavier. To act as counterweights, tear off tiny slips of metal foil and stick them inside the lighter portion of the cup. Keep adding small pieces until the assembly is balanced. It is very important that the assembly be evenly weighted all around.

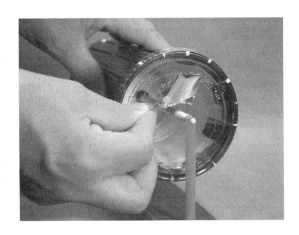

26. It is now time for the final test. Place the completed assembly directly under a lit 60-watt bulb, about 5 or 6 inches away. If the motor does not start turning immediately, give it a gentle push and it should continue to spin on its own. Do not let the motor sit under a light for extended periods of time if it is not turning.

27. Occasionally the cup assembly may become unbalanced. Add additional metal foil to act as a counterweight as needed. Store the assembly off the stand.

28. For advanced studies, additional weight can be added to the plastic lids to act as a flywheel. Wrap solder used for plumbing around a cup to bend it into a circular shape. Use a hot glue gun to permanently attach this additional mass to the plastic lid.

SAFETY NOTE
Be careful. Hot glue can burn fingers.

Instructional Information

Overview

To find what a can of soda would feel like on other planets, you can alter the contents of several containers to simulate the change in surface gravity according to the various planets. The cans can be passed around and students can feel how the same object would appear to feel "lighter" if it were taken to a planet with less gravity, or "heavier" if on a planet with more surface gravity, such as Jupiter. The set of cans and a few other simple props are helpful in clarifying why the mass of an object remains constant and is independent of gravity while the weight of the object can change according to locations.

Student Skills

Observation. The cans represent the differences in gravity that would be experienced by visiting our Moon and other planets. Give each student the opportunity to pick up the cans and feel the simulated differences in weight that each can represents.

Application and Writing. Students can determine their own weight—or the weight of a friend if they don't want to reveal their own—for each planet and describe what it might be like to live under such conditions.

Measurements. The cans can be used in differentiating between weight and mass of an object. Have students use balances and spring scales to make measurements. They should learn how these two measurements would differ in response to changes of gravity.

Related Concepts or Processes

Force   Weight
Mass   Gravity

Prior Knowledge

This set of cans makes an appropriate demonstration for students of all ages. Before showing the cans, make sure the youngest students have a basic understanding of some concepts about the planets and gravity. They should know that the planets are different sizes and that they all have gravity. Older elementary and middle school students should know that force is an effort applied against an object as a push or a pull. They should also have an idea that gravity is an attractive force exerted by all matter. They also may know that weight is a measure of the pull of gravity, that this force will decrease as a person moves away from the planet's surface, that there are several factors that can determine the amount of gravity felt on a planet, such as mass of the object, amount of mass of the planet, size of the planet, density of the planet, and location on the planet surface.

Predemonstration Discussion

Before using the cans, it might be helpful to review some concepts about weight and gravity. Some students may have a misconception that the atmosphere holds objects on the surface of a planet. Middle-school-age students may have learned that weight and mass of an object can be measured using different methods.

Some questions that might be helpful include the following:
- What holds objects on the surface of a planet?
- Is there gravity on other planets?
- What are some factors that determine the amount of gravity on a planet?
- What factors determine why someone might be heavier than someone else?
- Is there more gravity on the Earth or on the Moon?
- How is force measured and what are the metric units?
- What does the weight of an object actually tell us about that object?
- What are the units of mass?

Suggestions for Presentation

The cans can be used in different ways depending on the concept you want to show. They can be used to show how the pull of gravity might feel different from planet to planet. The cans are most useful when they lead into a discussion of gravity, of what factors might influence the pull of gravity, or of how to differentiate between weight and mass. Small planets or planets that are less dense than Earth may have less surface gravity; so an object on these planets would feel lighter. It is also possible that planets that are larger than Earth have less surface gravity because they are less dense than Earth (Uranus for example). Large dense planets would have more surface gravity than Earth; so an object there would feel heavier than here on Earth. To demonstrate the relative surface gravities on the various planets, pass the soda cans around for students to examine. Start with the "regular" can and have students lift it first as a reference. As the cans are passed around, discuss with students some possible reasons for a change in the weight from one planet to the next.

The cans can be identified with a choice of a few different types of labels. Give students a table listing the relative surface gravities of each planet. You can ask students to determine which can matches which planet. Students can heft the cans or use a balance to determine a ranking.

Another possibility is to label the cans with a mass (grams) and the metric unit of force (newtons). These labels are more applicable when trying to explain measuring the weight of an object using a spring scale versus measuring the mass of an object using a balance. After students have had an opportunity to examine the cans, you should use a spring scale and a balance to clarify this concept.

 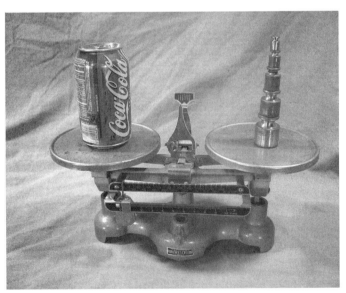

Measure the weight of the regular soda can using the spring scale as a demonstration. After discussing how the same can would feel on the Moon, measure the weight of the Moon's can using another spring scale and point out to the students that it is about $1/6$ of the measurement here on Earth. Hold the cans up side by side and again review why the spring scales would show two different readings. Remind students that the Moon can is a simulation.

After comparing the weight on the Earth and Moon, use a balance to measure the can again. This time you are measuring the mass. Focus a short discussion on the idea that the amount of matter contained in a real soda can would not change from one place to another.

Lead students toward an understanding that readings taken from the balance will not change from one planet to another. It is easier for students to follow the discussion if you place a soda can on one side of a balance and brass weights on the other side of the balance. Although the cans may feel lighter or heavier due to a change of location, it is very important to make clear that the brass pieces used to operate the balance will also change by the same percentage as they go from location to location with the soda can. This means the mass is not affected by a change in gravity. The balance will always indicate that the soda can equals the same number of grams (mass) no matter where it is measured.

Interactive questions during the presentation could include the following:
- Is there gravity on the Earth?
- Is there gravity on the Moon?
- If we took a can of soda up to the Moon, how would the can feel?
- How does the pull of gravity on the Moon compare to the pull of gravity on the Earth?
- If we were to weigh the can using a spring scale, how would it change going from one planet to another?
- Would there be a change in the weight of the cans as you traveled from one planet to another?
- Does the content of the can change if we go from one planet to another?
- If we took a balance to the Moon, how would the weights on the balance be affected by the change in gravity?
- Would there be a change in the mass of the cans as you traveled from one planet to another?

This demonstration does have limitations in how an object might "feel" in another location. When lifting against the pull of gravity, the cans represent how lifting an object might be changed according to a new location. What the cans do not represent accurately is other types of movements. Students might expect that other forces or inertia might change drastically also. This is where the cans will be misleading. The inertia depends on mass; the inertia of a can of soda or any other object would not be changed. It would still require the same amount of force to move the cans in horizontal directions. Newton's second law is not dependent on gravity. Acceleration and deceleration forces would not change. This could open up some interesting discussions.

Questions might include the following:
- Would a person be able to jump higher in less gravity?
- How might a long jump change in a stronger gravitational field?

- How might movement differ in a stronger gravitational field?
- Would someone be able to throw an object faster in a location having less gravity?
- Would catching objects be different on a planet with a small gravity field? How might it change; how would it be the same?

Postdemonstration Activities and Discussion

Have students make a table to demonstrate their understanding. The table should show the mass and also their calculated weight on each planet. Mass would be the same for each location; the weights will change according to the surface gravity.

Have students write a composition describing how living conditions would differ due to the amount of gravity and how might it feel and affect their movements.

Have students research ancient methods and units for measuring weight.

Students can also research official documents for descriptions of methods for measuring weight and mass. In some cases, government agencies may blur the distinction by not clearly indicating which unit they are describing.

Discussion of Results

The pull of gravity varies according to the size and density of a planet. The cans give students a glimpse of the changes in gravitational pull from one place to another. The amount of gravity is determined by the amount of matter that the planet contains. The pull of gravity is inversely proportional to the distance away from the center of the planet. Students can be questioned about this concept if it is appropriate.

The difference between weight and mass is a bit harder for students to comprehend. It also confuses many adults. Many people do not think that there is a difference between weight and mass, and it was not until we started our exploration of space that it was likely the average person would try to imagine what it must mean to be "weightless." The problem lies in that even though an object may be "weightless," it has not changed physically. It still has the same amount of matter.

If you ask for the weight of an object and then specify that you want the metric units, a large percentage of the public will give the units as grams instead of using newtons. Many students and adults have the misconception that mass and weight are interchangeable when measuring "the amount of matter in a substance." And in practice, they both are telling us how much matter is present.

Science textbook definitions of mass and weight can make the differences still seem a little vague to students. Isaac Newton defined mass as the quantity of matter; he referred to it as a measurement of the amount of inertia that an object has. Others may refer to it as the amount of matter in something. This definition seems to work with middle school students. It should be emphasized that mass is measured by comparing an object to standardized units that measure the amount of matter. The point should also be made that the mass is not dependent on location.

Most science book sources will define weight as a force measuring the gravitational pull of the planet where the object is located. The mass of an object is solely dependent on the amount of matter in the substance being measured.

We identify gravity as an attractive force that exists among all objects that have mass.

When we measure weight (force of gravity) we are measuring the pull of this attractive force. Three factors that influence the amount of gravity that an object feels include the following:

- the amount of matter or mass in the object (common to both types of measurements). Increase the mass and the weight goes up; cut the mass in half and the amount of gravity would be halved also.
- the amount of matter or mass of the planet. As the mass increases, the planet's gravity also increases. If the planet's mass were to double, so would its pull of gravity.
- the distance between an object and the center of the planet. As the distance between an object and the center of the planet grows, the force of gravity decreases rapidly. For example, if the distance between an object and a planet center were doubled, the force would only be ¼ of original measurement. Four times the distance would reduce the gravity to $1/16$ of the original amount. The force is reduced by the square of the distance between the object and the planet center.

In commercial and everyday use, the term *weight* is quite often used as a synonym for mass. Dictionaries can reveal the reason for this confusion. A definition for weight might say, "pertaining to finding the mass of." This certainly does not clear things up. Adding to the confusion is the objects that we put on a balance when we are measuring mass. These are usually referred to as "weights."

The best practice for the science classroom is to specify the measurement that is needed, the units that are desired, and the piece of equipment that should be used, as in the following examples:

- Find the weight of an object using the spring scale and measure to the nearest whole newton.
- Determine the mass of the matter using a balance and measure it to the nearest $1/10$ of a gram.

Additional Activities

Why is there a need to differentiate between weight and mass? Part of the need arises in the study of concepts such as motion, inertia, momentum, acceleration, and kinetic energy. Because weight is a force, students must be able to clearly distinguish and identify how forces differ from mass when using Newton's laws of motion. These three laws are the key to understanding how and why objects can move. Newton's first law tells us that the tendency of an object to resist changes in its state of motion is dependent upon mass. Inertia is a quantity that is solely dependent upon mass. The more mass an object has, the more inertia it has, and the more tendency it has to resist changes in its state of motion. The basis of Newton's second law demonstrates the relationship between force, mass, and acceleration.

To gain a better understanding and see how these measurements differ, students can find it helpful to observe devices measuring weight and mass under accelerated conditions.

If students have access to a building with an elevator, they can observe Newton's laws in action.

For the short time an elevator accelerates upward, a spring scale will momentarily measure an increase in force. Under the same conditions, a trip balance reading remains level and balanced indicating no change in mass. Students can also observe the results when the elevator stops on the ascent, starts to descend, and then stops on the descent.

If a camcorder is available, students can record their observations and narrate the apparent motions they are feeling compared to the observations on the measuring devices.

The elevator setup for the balance would have an object (full soda can) placed on one side of the double pan balance and brass weights on the other side. Adjust the amount of brass weights to make the 2 pans level. The balance sits on the floor of an elevator. Student observations should include:
• The balance shows no change during vertical acceleration or deceleration.
• The balance shows no change during steady up or down vertical velocity.

The spring scale placement in an elevator should have an object (full soda can) attached to the support hook of a spring scale. The spring scale must be attached to a steady support. A camera tripod makes an ideal frame for supporting the spring scale. Student observations should include the following:

- The spring scale shows an increase in force during the acceleration going up.
- A spring scale will read the same force in a motionless state or under steady up or down vertical velocity.
- A spring scale will momentarily show less force as it decelerates as the elevator comes to a stop when going up.
- The spring scale will momentarily show less force as an elevator starts down.
- The spring scale will momentarily show more force when the elevator slows to a stop on the descent.

Students can make the same observations as they stand on a spring-loaded bathroom scale. The scales must be the spring-loaded type; digital scales do not work for this demonstration.

If an elevator is not available, a simulated one is easily built. Materials needed include 20 feet of string, a pulley, and a piece of thin plywood. A spring scale and a balance will again show a difference in how they react to an accelerated motion. You might want to use an older double pan balance for this experiment in case the "elevator" lands too quickly.

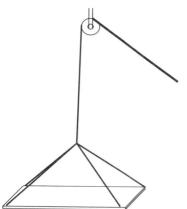

Attach the pulley to the ceiling on a support strong enough to handle the force applied to it. Attach the string to the four corners of the plywood and then a single strand to the pulley and off to the side.

Center the double pan balance on the piece of plywood. Place an object (such as a soda can) on one pan and balance it with brass weights on the other. Pull upward on the string and note that the balance does not alter its reading. Allow the elevator to drop—freefall is not suggested—a short distance. It still does not register a change in mass.

It may take some adjustment to make sure the balance is centered and then pulled straight upward. Don't let the elevator fall all the way to the floor.

The balance on the elevator simulator is shown here.

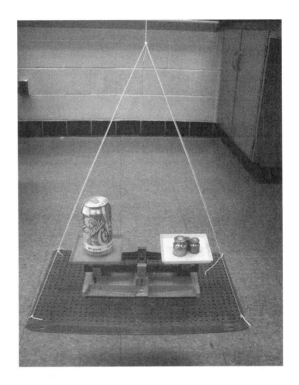

There are several designs of spring scales, and all of them will show changes in force due to vertical acceleration and deceleration of the soda can.

One type of spring scale that works well on the elevator was originally designed for measuring food. The scale's units were shown as ounces. The casing surrounding the dial face was removed and a new paper face was installed with units of newtons.

The same object (full soda can) can be placed on this spring scale, which is then placed on the simulated elevator.

Another possible setup is to use a dial-spring scale. In this case the plywood framing is not needed.

Replace the elevator with the spring scale, and hang the full soda can from the lower hook. It is not a good idea to attach the hook of the scale to the soda can tab, because quick accelerations will cause the soda can to open. You can tie string around the can and fasten it with plastic tape.

Once again, accelerate the object by lifting upward and note the changes on the scale during acceleration and then deceleration. Let it fall a short distance and note the effects.

Students can observe the spring scale drop to zero as the can is allowed to free-fall for a few feet.

Have students write an explanation to explain the difference between the balance and the spring scale reaction to vertical acceleration.

The balance remains unchanged during acceleration and deceleration for the same reason that a change in gravity does not affect it. The objects on either side of the balance have the same amount of mass. When the elevator accelerates or decelerates, both sides of the balance experience the same change of velocity. According to Newton's second law, the same acceleration or deceleration applied to the same amount of mass means that both objects "feel" the same force. The vertical forces acting on either side of the balance during acceleration and deceleration will always be equal, so the balance arm remains level.

The observations made on a spring scale caused by vertical acceleration are due to the nature of inertia and Newton's second law. When a spring scale supports a soda can, the scale will measure the amount of gravity pulling down on the soda can. When the soda can is accelerated upward, the inertia of the can resists any change to the motion. The spring scale indicates how much force is needed to overcome this inertia and accelerate the can upward. Newton's second law tells us that, to lift the elevator more quickly, more force will be needed as the rate of acceleration increases. After the soda can stops accelerating upward, the force on the spring scale registers the same as when the can was motionless. When the can decelerates on the ascent, the spring scale will indicate a decrease of force applied to the can. This is also due to inertia. The can is in motion upward, the force against the can is decreased, and the force of gravity overcomes the motion.

As the elevator accelerates down, less force is needed because gravity is already applying a force in that direction against the soda can. If the can is allowed to free-fall, the scale will read zero, indicating no force is being applied to the soda can except for the force of gravity pulling it down. As the soda can decelerates on the descent, the spring scale shows an increase in force until the can comes to a complete rest. Once the can comes to a complete stop, the only force shown on the spring scale will be the weight of the soda can.

Section 8

Directions for Assembly

Materials

- sand and lead fishing weights or 1,010 pennies

- aluminum foil tape or duct tape

- clear plastic tape

- 6–10 cans of soda, all the same brand and label

The directions offer a few variations of the assembly of the cans. The simplest method is to use empty soda cans. For a nicer look, keep the pop-top on the cans and empty the soda by making a hole in the bottom of the can.

Directions

1. The first step is to determine how many different planetary gravitational fields you wish to demonstrate. The Earth and the Earth's Moon plus a couple of other planets are usually enough to get the idea across.

   Next, decide how the cans will be emptied. The normal way is to pull the tab at the top and drink the contents. A nicer appearance will result from the cans' being emptied from the bottom.

144

2. If emptying the can from the bottom, use an ice pick or similar object to drive a small hole in the bottom of the can. A cloth or paper towel covering the bottom can keep the soda from spraying up.

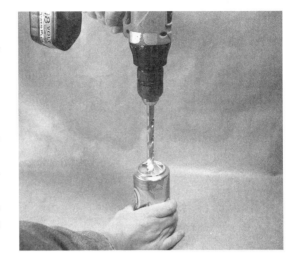

3. After it is emptied, use a large drill bit to enlarge the hole to fit the sinker/sand combinations or the alternative construction method that suggests using pennies. A ½-inch hole should work. It can be made longer using a screwdriver to accommodate the pennies.

   Do not empty all of the cans. Leave one intact to represent Earth.

   Each can is going to be filled with a combination of foam bits, sand, and, in Jupiter's case, lead weights. The sand and lead are needed to add the right amount of mass. The mass of each can and contents are listed on p. 148, Building Table Measurement for Building purposes.

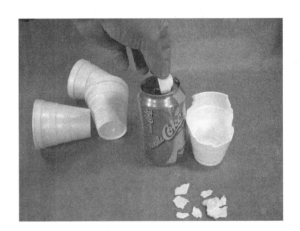

4. Add bits of foam to keep the can walls from being crushed during handling. Take several foam cups, and tear them into very small bits.

   Starting with the Mars can, add the bits of foam pieces through the hole in the can and fill it about ⁴/₅ of the way full. Put the can on the balance and check its mass.

Weigh Your Cans

5. Add a small amount of sand, but keep it less than 148 grams. Add more foam to the can, and add a bit more sand. The idea of this process is to get the can packed with foam and the right amount of sand so that it will have a mass of 148 grams. Pack the foam in as tightly as possible. Because the walls are thin, tightly packing the can gives them strength and keeps them from collapsing so easily.

6. Cut a piece of aluminum foil tape or duct tape and cover the hole in the can. Add a second piece of tape over the first piece to give it additional strength.

7. To make the rest of the cans, refer to the building table (p. 148) to determine the mass of each can. Repeat steps 4 through 10, except for Jupiter.

   Because Jupiter is such a massive planet, it has a gravitational pull about 2.6 times greater than Earth. Sand alone will not add enough mass to simulate this weight. The Jupiter can needs lead sinkers added to the mixture.

   To reach a mass of 889 grams, add enough lead weights to reach about 800 grams. The rest of the mass can be the mixture of sand and foam. Once again pack it as tightly as possible with the foam bits.

Alternatives to steps 5 through 7

You can use pennies as an alternative to the sand and lead weights. The table gives approximate numbers of pennies needed to build each can. For all 9 planets to be built would require about $10 in pennies.

Filling the can with bits of foam is helpful whether using sand and lead or pennies. The foam will help to keep the cans from being crushed during handling. If foam is added, the number of pennies should be decreased.

Because pennies can differ slightly in their mass, check the mass by adding the pennies and foam while the soda can is on the balance. Keep adding both until the correct mass is achieved.

To determine the correct mass for Jupiter accurately, you can measure the pennies in sections because the balance may not be able to handle all of the mass at once.

Cut out the planet name, mass, and weight for each can and then tape them somewhere on the side of the container for identification.

Weigh Your Cans

Building Table—Measurements for Building Purposes

Planet	Relative surface gravity	Total mass for building purposes	Approx. number of pennies needed
Sun	28	10.64 kilograms	4006
Mercury	0.38	144.4 grams	45
Venus	0.91	345.8 grams	121
Earth	1	380 grams	Soda in can
Moon	0.17	64.6 grams	15
Mars	0.38	144.4 grams	45
Jupiter	2.53	961.4 grams	354
Saturn	1.14	433.2 grams	154
Uranus	0.9	342 grams	120
Neptune	1.14	433.2 grams	154
Pluto	0.08	30.4 grams	2

Another possibility is to give each can a random number to conceal the identity. Students would have to use their measuring skills to determine the represented planet. Either can be printed on a computer printer and then cut out and taped to the side of the container.

Examples of labels to be taped onto the sides of the cans are shown.

Mercury	380 grams	1.4 newtons
Venus	380 grams	3.3 newtons
Earth	380 grams	3.7 newtons
Moon	380 grams	0.63 newtons
Mars	380 grams	1.4 newtons
Jupiter	380 grams	9.3 newtons
Saturn	380 grams	4.2 newtons
Uranus	380 grams	3.3 newtons
Neptune	380 grams	4.2 newtons
Pluto	380 grams	0.3 newtons

8. The cans are shown with the planet name, mass, and the weight measured in newtons. Note that the mass is given as 380 grams for each can. This is to demonstrate that the mass of the cans does not vary from location to location.

Instructional Information

Overview

You can observe this breakfast box sitting in plain view on a shelf, table, window ledge, or any other position that is remote enough to keep anyone from accidentally bumping against it. What is unusual about the box is that it is positioned with ¾ of the box hanging over the edge and just one corner supporting it. Why doesn't the box fall?

This prop can lend itself to discussions about levers or the center of gravity.

Student Skills

Inference. Without looking inside the box, students can infer that the center of gravity has been shifted to one side of the box.

Inference. Without looking inside the box, students can infer that the box can act as a first-class lever. The side supported on the shelf has a greater amount of torque than the side that is hanging over the edge.

Application. Have students identify the center of gravity in other structures or in handheld objects.

Application. Have students identify other situations that demonstrate balancing due to equal torques being applied to both side of a lever.

Research. Students can investigate how the center of gravity affects a variety of structures and objects.

Design and Construct. Students can build their own mobiles using the concepts discussed in this section.

Related Concepts or Processes

Center of gravity	Center of mass
Balanced or unbalanced	Area of support
Stability	Equilibrium
Levers	Torque

Prior Knowledge

The balanced box demonstration is appropriate for students in all grades. The idea of balancing objects and levers can be investigated in elementary school grades. Students should have been introduced to what is meant by balancing and that objects need support underneath them. They should also know that unbalanced objects would fall over or align themselves unless they have adequate support. One other concept that would help in the explanation of balancing objects is that gravity is a force that pulls down on all objects.

If this box is used to discuss levers, students should know that levers pivot around a fulcrum. Although they may not be able to identify the concept of torque, they may at least know that it is possible for two uneven masses to balance on a lever, a concept they may have already discovered by playing on a seesaw.

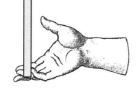

Predemonstration Discussion

The discussion that precedes the examination of the cereal box should depend on the age group.

Some initial activities might include showing various examples of situations that demonstrate objects being balanced.

A stick balanced on a hand can be a good example. Items that have a low center of gravity can be compared to long narrow objects that can upset very easily.

Some questions that might be asked include the following:
- What is meant by the term balanced?
- What is meant by the term unbalanced?
- Where must an object be supported to keep it from falling over?
- What determines when an object will fall over?
- How can we make an unbalanced object balanced?
- How is it possible for a heavy child and a light child to balance on a seesaw? Which child needs to be closer to the fulcrum?

Suggestions for Presentation

The setup of this prop has a few variations, but its essential purpose can be a lead-in for a lesson on the idea of center of gravity or it can be used to identify levers that are balanced about a pivot point. You should keep this box in an observable but inaccessible position for a few days before using it as a lesson prompt just to familiarize the students with the box and arouse their curiosity about its intended use. On the day of the lesson, place the box in a more prominent observable position with ¾ of the box hanging out over the ledge of the shelf or desk edge. The placement should be remote enough that students cannot accidentally bump it. As students observe it, do not allow anyone close enough to pick it up.

Interactive questions for discussion during the presentation could include the following:
- How do you think the box can stay on the shelf without falling?
- List three or four possible alternate possibilities for why the box does not fall over.

To help with a discussion about levers, a few examples can be set up to help students visualize the setup. The first example shows a meterstick with the fulcrum placed directly under the center position. A large mass is placed near the fulcrum, it is balanced by placing smaller mass farther away from the fulcrum. The second lever sets the fulcrum toward one end, and a mass is placed on the short end of the lever.

There is no mass placed on the longer end.

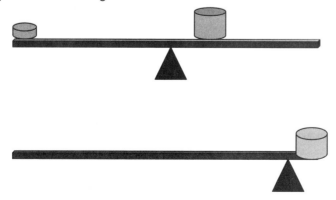

Lever 1:
- How is it possible to balance a light mass and the heavy mass on the meterstick?
- What would happen if both masses were the same distance away from the fulcrum?
- Does the meterstick have any mass?

Lever 2:
- How is it possible for the heavy weight to balance on the meterstick without any masses placed on the opposite side?
- What would happen if the fulcrum were moved toward the heavy mass?
- What would happen if the fulcrum were moved toward the center of the meterstick?
- Which lever setup do you think best represents what is occurring with the cereal box?

Postdemonstration Activities and Discussion

Discussions with students can involve why objects balance. It could include questions such as the following:
- Why do objects need support under the center of gravity?
- How can we locate the center of gravity?
- How does a double pan balance work?
- How is balance important to the design of furniture?
- How is balance important to the design of buildings?

Have students research the center of gravity problem occurring with the leaning tower of Pisa.
- What were the problems encountered when building the tower?
- What are some steps currently taken to resolve the problems?

• A series of books can be stacked in such a way that one of the books is completely over the edge. If they are extended too far over the edge they will fall to the floor. How is the balancing of these books similar to the plight of the leaning tower of Pisa?

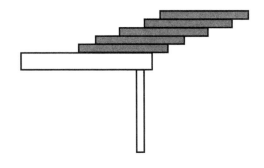

The simplest way to find the center of gravity of an object is to find a position where it will balance on the fingers.

Another way to determine the center of gravity is shown in the picture at the right. It is a bit more complicated. Start with an irregularly shaped object and drill a few small holes somewhere on the outside perimeter. Hang the object from one hole and then drop a weighted string from the same position. Draw a line on the object along the string.

Repeat the procedure from another hole on the object drawing a second line on the object. The center of gravity is the point where the lines intersect.

This procedure works well for irregularly shaped objects cut out of plywood or cardboard. The object will balance on the finger at the intersection of these two lines.

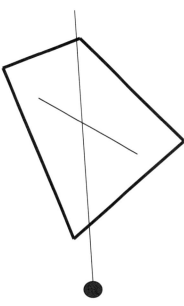

If You Build It, They Will Learn

Balanced Breakfast Box

A set of common geometric and irregularly shaped boards can be made out of cardboard or plywood for students to test. Repeat a few of the shapes and glue an additional weight such as a lead sinker or wood block to move the position of the center of gravity.

Draw the shapes on a piece of paper as a handout for students. Ask them to make predictions about the location of the center of gravity. Have students use a string and weight to locate the actual position and compare their finding to the predictions. With a little practice students center can balance these shapes on a finger at the identified center of gravity.

Discussion of Results

The force of gravity and where the box is being supported determines the balancing of this box. It must have support under a location known as the center of gravity. If this position is not supported, the box will fall over. The center of gravity can be the geometric position of any object, and most people would suspect that it is located in the center when they look at a cereal box. The assumption is that cereal bits remaining in the box are spread evenly throughout it. Obviously, that is not the case with this box. The center of gravity is the average location of the applied force of gravity of an object. By adding the very large mass to one side, the center of gravity has been shifted from the center to the extreme right side.

The picture shows the box with the front panel cut away. Think of the box as a lever and the edge of the shelf as the fulcrum. To illustrate this better, place a small block underneath the box at a position where it is a balanced lever: The block is the fulcrum. This position occurs because the heavy mass is applying a clockwise torque to the box on the right side of the wooden block. Most of the box and a small portion of the heavy mass are applying a counterclockwise torque on the left side of the block. The box balances when these two torques are equal.

With a little practice students can balance these shapes on a finger at the identified center of gravity. An interesting question is if it would be possible to balance the box on the very edge? It is, but the box must be tilted.

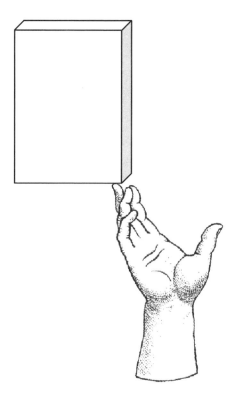

Additional Activities

Using some scraps of wood and string, students can investigate how the forces and distances must be adjusted to make objects balance. Mobiles can be quite simple or involve several levels, adding to their complexity. These mobiles can be hung from the ceiling and can be used in the discussions of balanced forces, torque, and levers. They make a nice permanent display in any classroom.

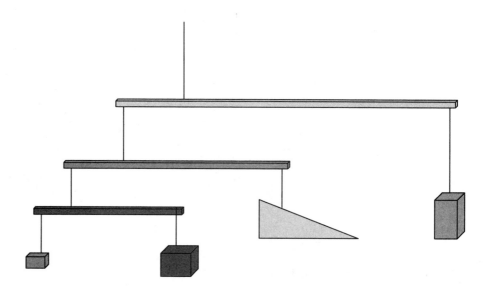

Directions for Assembly

Materials

- cereal box, such as Cheerios or Wheaties

- 1 kg mass heavy weight, either divers weight, empty soda can filled with sand, or other suitable heavy object

- adhesive materials, silicone glue, double sided tape, or duct tape

Directions

1. Select an empty cereal box that is wide enough for the heavy mass to fit snuggly into the bottom corner.

   Because cereal box cardboard is not very strong, use an additional piece of cardboard to reinforce the bottom of the box.

2. Cut out a piece of cardboard that is narrow enough to fit inside the box. The length should be about 8 to 10 inches. Fold the cardboard so that one side of it is as long as the side of the heavy weight.

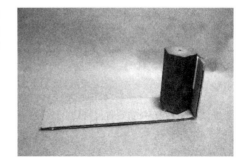

3. Start by applying the silicone glue liberally to the side and bottom of the weight, and then press the weight firmly in place on the folded cardboard. Allow it to dry completely before proceeding. A less permanent procedure is to use double-sided tape or duct tape to join the cardboard and weight together.

4. The last step is to adhere the weight and cardboard inside the cereal box.

   Apply liberal amounts of glue to the cardboard reinforcement, and then place it into the inside corner of the cereal box. Press the glued portion firmly into place.

   A less permanent procedure is to use tape to attach the weight and cardboard combination to the inside of the cereal box.

5. A soda can filled with sand can be an alternative to the heavy metal weight but does not work quite as well. Using a heavy metal weight allows the box to be hung over the edge a bit further.

6. The box is shown with a soda can inside.

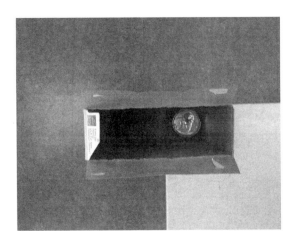

7. Position the box with the weighted side on the edge of a table or shelf.

Instructional Information

Overview

How good are you at judging the weight of an object? In this demonstration, a person holds a large foam board and a small brass weight to compare their respective weights. After hefting both objects for a few moments, the person is asked to determine which is heavier. According to the senses, the obvious answer is the brass. When the objects are compared using a balance or a lever, the startling results show that the foam is the heavier object. This simple test fools 90% of those who try it, illustrating that it's better to rely on quantitative methods when comparing the weight of objects.

Student Skills

Observation. Students can learn that an object that feels heavier may not be heavier.

Application. Students should be able to identify a variety of other situations where pressure is determined by the amount of surface area against the ground.

Measurements and Calculations. Students can determine the pressure by calculating the area of the surfaces and dividing it into the applied force.

Draw a Conclusion. Students can draw conclusions about the relationship between surface area and pressure. They can also make conclusions about the relationship between mass, volume, and the density of an object.

Related Concepts or Processes

Weight   Mass
Gravity   Pressure
Forces   Density

Prior Knowledge

This demonstration is appropriate for students at all levels. It can be used with elementary students after they have been introduced to the concept of weight and forces. The idea of some objects being "heavier" than others can be shown to first- and second-graders, and some simple discussion can follow explaining why. Older students should have some background knowledge about forces, gravity, and density.

Predemonstration Discussion

Questions could include the following:
- What does weight depend on?
- What causes weight?
- Why are some things heavier than others?
- How do we measure the weight of an object?

Presentation

This demonstration is more effective when you seem to be comparing the foam and brass as a random act. The foam and brass piece should be sitting unobtrusively somewhere in the room.

This simple presentation begins when you ask a student to demonstrate his or her ability to act as a double-pan balance. Place random objects on the student's hands, and ask him or her to judge which is heavier. Then ask the student to make judgments about several sets of similarly sized objects before trying the foam and brass.

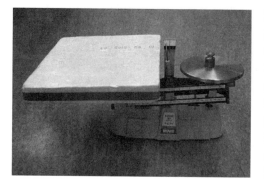

Place the brass in one hand and the foam in the other. Once again ask the student which is heavier. After this student has given his or her answer, ask a second student to verify the answer. Most likely several more students will ask to try these pieces and give their opinion. After students have had the opportunity to compare the foam block and the brass, ask them to verify their answers using a balance. Put the brass on the balance first and then add the foam to the opposite side. Students should have a clear view of the balance and see that the foam is slightly heavier than the brass.

Some students may have a misconception that the orientation of the foam block can make a difference when it is placed on the balance. You can place the block on the balance in a few different positions to show them orientation makes no difference in the weight.

Interactive questions for discussion during the presentation could include the following:
- If one object has more matter than another, which one should be heavier?
- What does weight depend on?
- What is weight?
- If two objects have the same amount of mass, how should the weight compare?
- Why would the foam weigh more or less than the brass weight?
- What does this tell us about the matter that is found in these pieces?
- How can we verify that one is heavier than the other?
- How do you explain the results observed on the balance?
- Does the orientation of the foam make a difference in measuring its weight?
- What does the demonstration suggest about using ones hands as a way of comparing or measuring matter?

The primary purpose of the foam-block-and-brass-weight device is to use it as an introduction to making measurements of materials, comparing the vast difference in densities of matter, or demonstrating pressure. A few additional ways of demonstrating the limitations of using the body's senses are suggested below. These can be used to reinforce the importance of making accurate measurements. For lower level students, dwell less on the inaccuracy of the body response than on the need for making accurate measurements.

Postdemonstration Activities and Discussion

The original activity can be used as an introduction into a few different areas of study. Some suggested areas include the application of pressure, measurement of weight and volume, and a comparison of these measurements in the calculating densities. The activity also demonstrates that hefting an object has severe limitations and cannot always be relied on. A more accurate method for measuring and comparing the weight of an object is using a balance and making a quantitative measurement. The body's senses in this case are not good judges for comparing these materials. The pressure exerted by the foam is spread over a large area of the palm. The hand does not recognize the amount of force spread out over a large area as easily as it does the same amount of force applied in a small area.

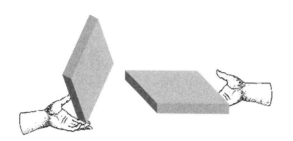

Try holding the foam in different positions and feel the difference. When the foam is oriented with the tiny edge pressing against the palm, it will feel much heavier.

The same object held in different positions will appear to be heavier or lighter, depending on the orientation. In this case, a roll of coins or a metal cylinder held on end feels heavier than when it is hefted on its side. Even different positions on the arm make a difference. An object placed on the arm near the elbow does not feel as heavy as the same object held in the hand.

This demonstration using the weight and foam can lead to a discussion of density. Students can measure the mass of the objects and then divide by the volume. The foam has an approximate density of about 0.1 grams per milliliter. The brass has an approximate density of 8.9 grams per milliliter. Classroom discussion should question why some objects are denser than others.

Have students measure the pressure that is exerted by each piece as it sits in the hand. Start by finding the force (weight) of both pieces. This can be done by measuring with a spring scale or by multiplying the mass by 9.8. Have students come up with methods of determining how much surface area each piece presses against the hand. One student suggested covering the hand with tempera paint and then measuring the outline left on the foam.

Discussion of Results

The brass weight is roughly 90 times denser than the foam material. When the brass is placed in the hand, it applies all of its weight (force) to a very small area of the hand. Force per area is measured as pressure. If the applied force stays the same but the area gets smaller, the pressure is said to increase. Inversely, if the force stays the same but the area of contact increases, the pressure is decreased.

Give the formula for measuring force:

$$Pressure = \frac{Force}{Area\ of\ Application}$$

Why does this experiment fool the body's senses? The physiological response of the body to stimuli is extremely complex. In theory, the limitation of the brain in identifying correctly which object weighs more may be due to conflicting data from a variety of sources. The nerves in the hands respond to pressure and elicit a stronger response to a large pressure applied in a small area rather than a smaller pressure over a large area, even when the total amount of applied force remains the same. An example of this is how the hand responds to a pinprick compared to how it responds to a blunt object lightly touching the skin. The pinprick is much more noticeable and the brain's response is vastly different.

Another potential source of conflicting information to the brain may be slightly different tensions exerted by the muscular/skeletal framework required for each piece. Visual cues from the eyes recognize the foam as a larger object that "should be" heavier. Show two different-sized unknown objects to a student, and he or she will suggest that the larger one will probably be heavier. This may be in direct conflict with another preconceived notion of metals' being heavier than other types of materials. All of these considerations, and possibly others, help the brain recognize and identify external stimuli and choose what it thinks is the appropriate response to them. As shown, the choice is not always accurate.

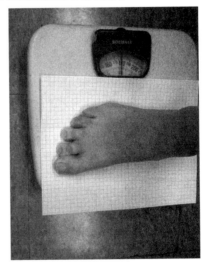

Additional Activities

Students can pursue additional studies and applications of pressure. For example, how much pressure does a person's foot exert when walking? Calculations can be made for a bare foot or the sole of a shoe.

To determine the pressure exerted by a bare foot, the force exerted and the area of application are needed for the calculations.

Start by having a volunteer step on a bathroom scale. You can place a paper on the scale for sanitary purposes. All of the volunteer's weight should be on one foot. Measure the reading of weight on the scale. In this case, the reading is 180 pounds.

Next, an accurate estimation of the area of the foot is needed. This can be accomplished with some ¼-inch graph paper and a bit of tempera paint. The paint should be watered down; it needs only enough pigment to stain the paper. Place the paint in a large plastic tray.

Have the volunteer step into the container of paint; only deeply enough to wet the bottom of the foot. Allow the excess paint to drip back into the paint tray.

Have the volunteer step firmly onto the center of the graph paper with full weight on the foot. After a few moments, lift the foot off of the paper.

After waiting for a few minutes for the paint to dry, determine the area of the bottom of the foot. Since the graph paper is measured in ¼-inch grid, the area is easily calculated as square inches.

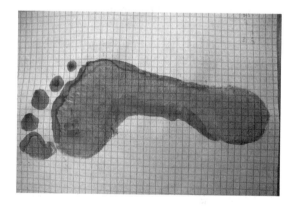

A ¼ inch-grid on the graph paper will yield 16 blocks per square inch. To determine the number of square inches of the foot, count up the number of blocks that are colored by the paint. You will need to estimate because some of the blocks will not be completely filled.

This footprint covers approximately 334 blocks.

The area of the footprint is found using the following formula:

Square inches = $\dfrac{\text{number of blocks}}{16}$ = $\dfrac{334}{16}$ = 20.9 sq.in.

The amount of pressure exerted by our volunteer's foot is found using the following formula:

Pressure = force = 180 lbs = 8.6 pounds per square inch (approximate)
           area   20.9 sq.in.

Typical examples for footprint pressure ranges from 7 to 11 pounds per square inch but can vary according to body type, shoe size, and arch type.

When discussing pressure, one of the most common examples is the large force exerted by a woman's stiletto-heeled shoe. The pressure is impressive and can easily be calculated. Of course, the first thing needed is a volunteer with a pair of high-heeled shoes, the smaller the diameter of the heel, the better.

This demonstration follows the same directions given for the bare foot. Tell students that a person momentarily supports all of her weight on each heel during the process of walking. There are times when the heel will be generating the pressure calculated below.

The example shown at the right shows the impression left by a 110-pound volunteer with high heels.

The imprint of the heel is approximately 3 blocks. This yields an area of 0.19 square inches for the heel portion of the shoe. The amount of pressure exerted by the heel is calculated by the following:

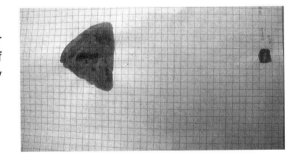

Pressure = force = 110 lbs = 579 pounds per square inch
           area   0.19 sq.in.

With this kind of pressure, it's easy to understand why stiletto heels can leave indentions in some types of flooring material.

Other examples of "footprints" can be compared and calculated. For example, why do mountain bikes have large wide tires and road bikes have very skinny tires. And, why do the mountain bike tires need less air pressure than the skinny road bike tires?

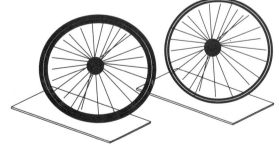

The pressure exerted by bike tires can be calculated in the same way suggested for feet and shoes. It can be compared to the pressure indicated by a tire pressure gauge.

Have a person sit on a bicycle and place the front wheel of a bicycle tire on a bathroom scale. Take a reading of the weight of the bicycle and rider.

This reading shows 92 pounds on the bathroom scale.

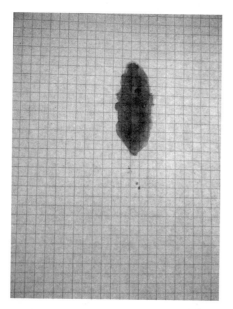

Determine the area of the front tire using graph paper and paint. Have the same person who sat on the bicycle when it was weighed sit on the bicycle with the painted tire pressed down against the graph paper.

The graph paper indicates 31 blocks covered with paint.

Area in square inches = $\frac{26}{16}$ = 1.6 square inches

Pressure = $\frac{force}{area}$ = $\frac{92\ lbs}{1.6\ sq.in.}$ = 57.5 pounds per square inch

Ideally, the air pressure inside the tire should match the calculated pressure that is exerted against the ground. Check the air pressure using a tire gauge. It can be measured without a person on the bike and then again with a person on the bicycle. The air pressure inside the tire will remain the same whether someone is sitting on the bicycle or not.

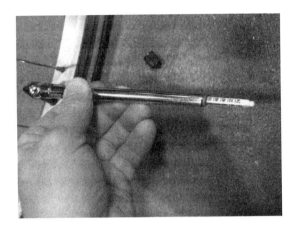

When the air pressure is measured with a tire gauge, it reads 55 pounds per square inch. The calculated pressure is 57.5 pounds per square inch. These are very reasonable results considering the equipment used to make the measurements.

A minibed of nails can also demonstrate pressure.

The board on the left has 64 nails driven through the bottom. They are ½ inch apart in each direction. The board on the right has a single nail driven through the bottom. A balloon can be pushed down against the bed of nails with quite a bit of force without it breaking. When the same balloon is pushed down against the single nail, it will break with very little effort. The pointed surface area of the single nail exerts a very large pressure against the balloon and easily penetrates the material to pop it.

SAFETY NOTE
Wear safety gloves during this demonstration.

Directions for Assembly

Materials

- 1 Styrofoam block, 1½ in. thick, 10 in. × 11 in.

- 1 100 g weight or a 2 oz. to 4 oz. lead fishing weight

The heavy object suggested for this experiment is a 100-gram brass weight that is used with a variety of balances. If this weight is not available, a large lead fishing weight is a good replacement. These are available any place that fishing tackle is sold. If a lead weight is used, it should be painted with two coats of a suitable paint to completely seal the lead metal.

The size of the foam block is dependent on the mass of the metal object.

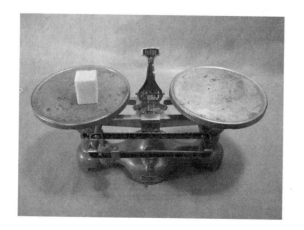

Directions

1. Measure the mass of the metal object using a balance.

   If 1½-inch foam insulation is used, cutting out a 1-inch square and measuring its mass can determine the size needed for this demonstration. A 1-inch square of foam has a mass of approximately 1 gram.

2. Determine the number of square inches of foam needed to give a mass equal to the metal object and add an additional 1 to 2 square inches to that number.

3. Mark out the number of square inches needed from the foam insulation supply.

   A serrated steel knife will do an adequate job of cutting the foam, and an electric carving knife works very well.

4. After cutting the foam insulation to the approximate size needed, measure its mass using a balance. The foam should be slightly heavier than the metal object. If the foam is more than 2 grams heavier than the metal mass, cut thin slivers of foam off until the desired mass is reached.

5. If the mass of the foam is slightly less than the metal object, some plastic tape can be wrapped around the perimeter of the block to make it heavier. An additional benefit to adding the tape is that it helps protect the edges of the foam.

6. The foam and the brass should be placed on a balance. The balance should show that the foam is slightly heavier than the metal object.

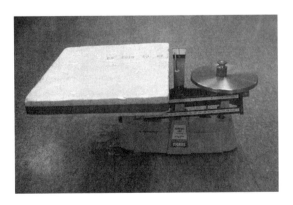

Instructional Information

Overview

Small wooden or cardboard boxes hang about 5 feet from the ceiling on a short length of string. A second string comes out of the bottom of the boxes. The purpose of the boxes is not immediately clear because the inner workings are hidden from view. A slight downward pull on the lower string, however, will cause the boxes to climb upward on the support strings. If the contents of the boxes are kept hidden, you can challenge students to make simple measurements and offer testable solutions on the action of each box.

Student Skills

Measurements. Students can try measuring the ratio of the upward distance that the box moves and compare it to the distance needed to pull down on the string. This can help them to determine the mechanical advantage of the system.

Trial and Error. The purpose of the mystery boxes is to challenge students to attempt their own version of it or at least determine a successful explanation of how it works. This may require them to test several designs before coming up with a design that works.

Design and Construct. After students have solved the inner workings of a mystery box, encourage them to build their own version and then put it on display within the classroom.

Inference and Application. Students should be able to identify that the box has simple machine parts inside to gain a mechanical advantage. With the workings hidden, they will not have direct evidence of the specific type, but they can look and listen for clues that might give them ideas. They can look for similar relationships of how applied forces change the direction and speed of devices in other types of simple machines.

Related Concepts or Processes

Simple machines   Inference

Indirect observations   Simple and compound machines

Mechanical advantage   Pliers

Wheel and axle   Force

Efficiency

Prior Knowledge

This piece of equipment is appropriate for upper elementary school students and above. It uses a change in the ratio of force to distance to accomplish its movement. Before introducing it to students, make sure they have some understanding of the concept of force. They also should be able to recognize and identify types of simple machines. Students should understand that a simple machine could change the direction of an applied force, the amount of force applied, the distance the force will be exerted, and the speed of the object against which the force was applied. In addition, students should be able to measure and identify input and output forces using a spring scale and be able to measure and identify input and output distances using a ruler.

Predemonstration Discussion

Rather than using the mystery box to introduce simple machines and mechanical advantage, use it as a supplemental piece after students have a working knowledge of the six types of simple machines. You can put this piece on display for several days during a unit on work and machines.

Questions and discussion for students before showing the box could include the following:
- Explain how a force can change to get a mechanical advantage.
- If force is increased by a simple machine, describe the effect this will have on the distance and speed as it applies to moving an object.
- How do we identify input forces and output forces?
- How can we identify and measure input and output distances?

SAFETY NOTE

If you hang the mystery boxes from a ceiling, make sure there is adequate support where the boxes are attached; students tend to pull harder on the cord than they need to. If you are tying to a tile ceiling support, check above the tile to find a location where the metal track is attached to the building structure.

Suggestions for Presentation

You can present these pulley boxes to students in several different ways. The operation can be in plain view or it can be hidden. You should hang the boxes in plain view from the ceiling or some other type of support. Pull down on the string, and each will climb upward. Allow students to try their hand at the movement.

If the workings of the pulley boxes are open and exposed, their operation can still be discussed and measured as a class demonstration. Some questions that can be discussed during the showing of the demonstration include the following:

- What measurements can we make on the movement of the boxes?
- What does a mechanical advantage indicate?
- What does a mechanical advantage of one indicate?
- What does a mechanical advantage that is greater than one indicate?
- How do we know if the arrangement inside requires a mechanical advantage to operate?
- Why is there a difference between the distances the box moves and how far the string has to be pulled down?
- Compare the weight of the box with how much force is needed to make it move (use spring scales). Why is one measurement more than the other?
- What is the efficiency of the device?
- Which box shows a greater mechanical advantage?

Perhaps the most effective way to use these boxes is to hang a couple of different types in the classroom when you start a unit on work and simple machines. Keep the boxes on display for several days, but keep the movements hidden. Students normally do not require any encouragement to try moving the boxes for themselves. At some point in your lessons on simple machines, discuss the boxes and how they fit into what your class is studying. Some questions that might be discussed during this lesson might include the following:

- What observations can we make about the box?
- What can we infer about the inside by measuring the outside?
- What measurement can we make on the movement of the box?
- How do we know if the arrangement inside requires a mechanical advantage to operate?
- Why is there a difference in the distance the box moves and how far the string has to be pulled down?
- Compare the weight of the box with how much force is needed to make it move (using spring scales). Why is one measurement more than the other?
- Calculate the efficiency of each box and compare.

Postdemonstration Activities and Discussion

Have students draw hypothetical diagrams of what might be set up inside the boxes. They should explain the function of each part and how the parts would function together to make a box move.

Have students make up a situation in which this mechanism would be useful.

Discussion of Results

The movement of the wood-framed mystery box is dependent on the differences in the pulley size as compared to the axle size. The box has a wheel-and-axle mechanism inside. A wheel and axle is a simple machine consisting of a large wheel rigidly secured to a smaller wheel identified as the axle. When either the wheel or axle is turned, the other part must also turn. If the wheel turns and the axle remains stationary, it is not considered to be a wheel-and-axle machine. This box moves upward because the force applied by the lower string is increased as the upper string wraps around the axle. The force increases because the distance the box moves is not as long as the distance the string is pulled. The action is a trade-off: A gain in force is accompanied by an appropriate loss of distance. This trade-off is identified as a mechanical advantage and is calculated as the ratio of radius of the wheel to the radius of the axle. The larger ratio of wheel to axle will make it easier to move the box upward.

A disadvantage to using a large ratio between the wheel and the axle is that, as the mechanical advantage is increased, the string must be pulled farther to raise the box the same distance. Calculating the mechanical advantage for the wheel and axle found inside the box is fairly simple. Assuming that the wooden wheel in the box has a radius of 1 inch and the axle has a radius of ¼ inch, the ratio of wheel to the axle residing inside the mystery box would be 4. This mechanical advantage applies to the wheel and axle only if the box is held stationary and the wheel and axle rotate at a fixed location.

The unusual operation of this wheel and axle is that it lifts itself as part of the resistance rather than remaining in a fixed position. As you pull down on the string, the box with the wheel and axle inside is moving up away from your hand. Because of this action, the mechanical advantage cannot be calculated as a simple wheel-and-axle ratio. The strings are wound opposing each other. When the wheel string is pulled down and unwinds, the axle string lifts the box upward by winding up. This exposes 25% more string coming out of the box than if the box remained in a fixed position. The radius of wheel is 1 inch, giving it a circumference of 6.28 inches. The radius of the axle is ¼ inch, giving it a circumference of 1.57 inches. Grab the string at the large wheel right at the surface of the box and pull down for a distance of 4.71 inches (¾ the circumference of the wheel). This will make the box move upward for a distance of 1.57 inches (circumference of the axle). The hand will be a distance of 6.2 inches away from the surface of the box, because the box moves up 1.5 inches as your hand moves down 4.7 inches.

The mechanical advantage of the mystery box has to be calculated by dividing the distance the force is applied by the distance the box moves rather than a ratio of the wheel-to-axle radius.

$$\frac{4.71 \text{ inches}}{1.57 \text{ inches}} = 3$$

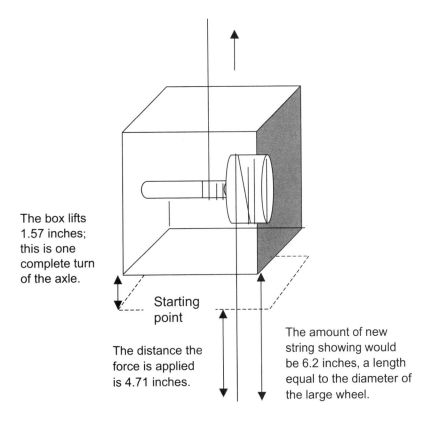

The box lifts 1.57 inches; this is one complete turn of the axle.

Starting point

The distance the force is applied is 4.71 inches.

The amount of new string showing would be 6.2 inches, a length equal to the diameter of the large wheel.

You can calculate the work done on or by any system by multiplying the force times the distance. When the work output of this box is divided by the work put into the box, the box's efficiency is about 80%. That means there is quite a bit of friction within this system. This could be improved with the use of bearings, but this improvement is not in the construction yet.

The movement of the cardboard-sided box is quite a bit simpler; it demonstrates a mechanical advantage of one. This example does not change the force against the box or distance the box moves compared to the distance the force is applied. The movement on this box is dependent on the washer's acting as a crude pulley. Compare this to a simple pulley setup, and you can see that the resistance force is the box itself.

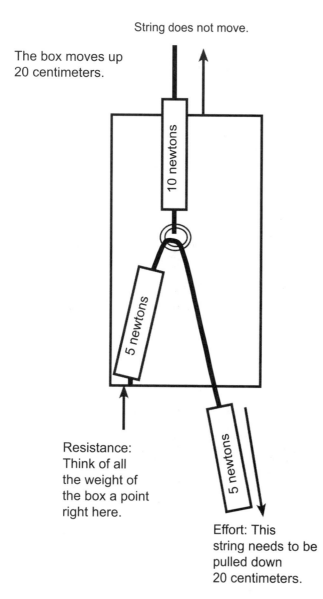

String does not move.

The box moves up
20 centimeters.

10 newtons

5 newtons

Resistance:
Think of all
the weight of
the box a point
right here.

5 newtons

Effort: This
string needs to be
pulled down
20 centimeters.

The string going into the box has a force applied to it. After this string loops through the washer, it then applies this force to the box frame. If the weight of the box is 5 newtons, the force applied to the string would also have to be 5 newtons. To raise the box 20 centimeters, the string is pulled down 20 centimeters. Note that pulling the string 20 centimeters will result in a total of 40 centimeters of string below the box. The box moves upward 20 centimeters, exposing the additional 20 centimeters of string.

Additional Activities

Because students are not shown the insides of the boxes, the boxes are a good extra-credit challenge for individuals or groups of students. Students can be challenged to build their own mystery box that performs in the same manner as the ones shown. The two requirements they must strictly adhere to:

The box must go up at least ⅓ the height of the box when the string is pulled and return down when released.

The box must be covered completely to hide is workings from other students and must not be revealed.

Students are very good at coming up with their own version of other types of mystery boxes. Encourage them to make other types of hidden movement devices and present them to the rest of the class. The class can then work in groups to design possible models that explain these other mysteries.

Directions for Assembly

Wooden Box
Materials

- 2 pieces of wood, 4 × 9 × 1 in.

- 2 pieces of wood, 4 × 6 × 1 in.

- 1 wood scrap, 1.5 in. thick heavy-duty nylon string

- 8 drywall screws

- 2 pieces of plywood 6 × 10.5 × ¼ in. thick (front and back cover are optional)

- 1 wooden dowel, ½ in. diameter × 5.5 in. long

To keep the workings and the operation of this pulley box hidden, make sure the axle for the pulley does not protrude through the sides of the box.

Directions

1. To start, cut and sand the 4 sides of the box frame. The side dimensions should be approximately 4 inches by 9 inches. The top and bottom plates are 4 inches by 6 inches.

2. To locate the position for the axles, find the center of the longer pieces by using a ruler to draw diagonal lines from opposite corners on each of 4-inch-by-9-inch wood pieces.

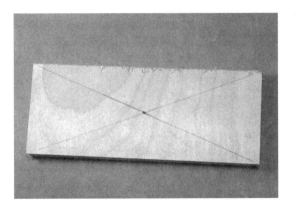

SAFETY NOTE

For this series of instructions, the following safety equipment is strongly recommended:

Goggles for eye protection. NSTA recommends that you use safety goggles that conform to the ANSI Z87.1 standard and that provide both impact and chemical-splash protection for all science laboratory work.

Dust mask to guard against breathing in airborne sawdust.

Gloves whenever power tools are used.

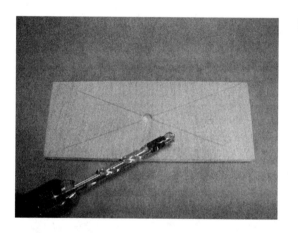

3. The holes for the axle are ½ inch in diameter and are drilled ½ inch deep into both 4-inch-by-9 inch blocks. Stick a piece of tape on the drill bit to mark the depth of how deep to drill. Do not drill all the way through the wood.

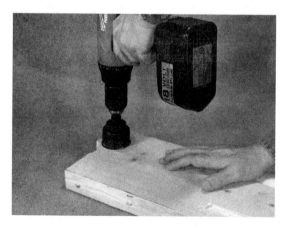

4. Cut the pulley wheel for the center of the mystery box from a 2-by-4 scrap stud. The diameter of the cylinder can range from 2 to 3 inches or larger. If a hole saw is not available, use a saber saw to cut out the wheel. An alternative is a wood spool used for thread.

5. The center of the wood cylinder must be drilled to the same diameter as the wooden dowel. Hold the cylinder in a vise. If a vise is not available, wear work gloves when holding the cylinder.

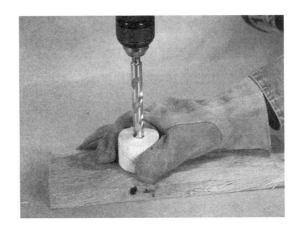

6. To make the pulley wheel, the wood cylinder must have larger diameter sides added. They should extend out at least ½ inch beyond the cylinder. Cut them out using a drill saw or a small handsaw.

7. An alternative to wooden sides for the pulley wheel can be made out of plastic or cardboard.

   A lid from a plastic container or cardboard from a box can be cut into a circular shape that is slightly larger than the diameter of the cylinder. Cut the center out of the disk so that it will fit onto the ½-inch wooden dowel.

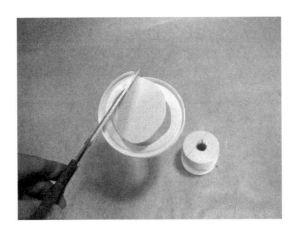

8. If plastic walls are used for the pulley wheel, they will need to be attached with small screws or nails. This type of plastic does not work very well with glue. If cardboard is used, it can be glued onto the sides of the cylinder.

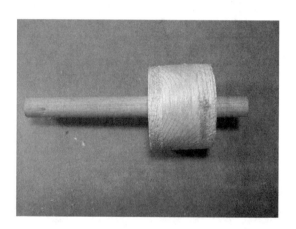

9. The wheel is mounted onto a 5.5-inch-long, ½-inch diameter wood dowel. Glue this cylinder onto this dowel. The position is 1 inch in from one of the ends.

10. The disks shown were cut from ¼-inch plywood. Slide these disks over the dowel and screw or glue them to the sides of the cylinder to hold them in place.

11. The string must be attached to the inside of the pulley wheel. One method is to drill a small hole through the side of the disks glued to the cylinder. If you use plastic or cardboard sides, you can screw a small eyehook into the cylinder portion of the pulley wheel.

12. The next step is constructing the frame using simple overlapping joints.

The top and bottom pieces of the frame will be screwed into the sidewalls. The shorter pieces are used for the top and bottom. Drill 4 pilot holes into the top plate and the bottom plate in preparation for joining the frame together.

13. The top and bottom plates overlap the sidewalls and must be joined together with screws. To do this, hold one of the sidewalls vertically and then match the edge of the smaller block of wood to the side edge of the sidewall. Make sure that the sidewall is used with the hole toward the inside of the box frame. Hold this block in place and screw the screws down into the wood. Two screws are needed for each of the 4 joints.

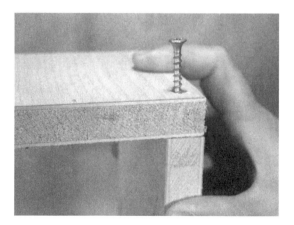

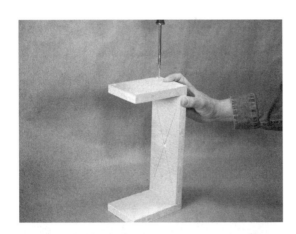

14. Turn the piece upside down so that the joint is now on the bottom, and add the other short piece to the frame. Once again, match up the edge of the short piece to the edge of the side-wall. Hold the short piece in place and screw the drywall screws down into the wood.

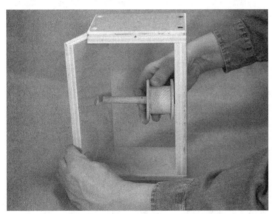

15. Insert the wood dowel assembly into the hole on the sidewall. With the dowel in place, slide the second side into position. The dowel should fit into the hole on the second side. This side piece is also overlapped by the top and bottom plates.

   Before screwing the drywall screws into the top and bottom to complete the frame, check to see that the dowel assembly turns freely in the support holes. If it does not, take the dowel assembly out of the frame and sand or cut the ends slightly until it does.

16. Measure the interior length of the dowel to locate the center. At the center position on the dowel, drill a ⅛-inch hole. This hole should be big enough for the string to be threaded through.

17. Determine which side will be the top of the box and drill a $3/16$-inch hole in this piece. The hole should be exactly in the center and should match up with the hole in the center of the axle.

18. Turn the frame over to drill a $^3/_{16}$-inch hole through the bottom plate. Position this hole over the center of the large cylinder so that the string will wind and unwind on the pulley wheel. This side of the box will be the bottom.

19. Cut off an 8-foot section of string and knot one end. Thread the other end of this string through the small hole drilled into the side-wall of the disk glued to the cylinder. Thread the string toward the cylinder and then wind it several turns around the large cylinder. Continue with this string by threading it through the hole in the bottom plate.

20. Cut off a 5-foot piece of string and tie a knot on one of the ends. Thread the opposite end though the hole drilled into the center of the axle. Then thread this end of the string up through the hole in the top plate.

21. Tie a loop on the end of the string coming out of the top of the box. This loop will be used to hang the box on some type of hook when the box is completed.

22. Hang the box on a support and pull down on the string coming out of the bottom of the frame. The frame should go upward as the bottom string is pulled down.

23. The mystery box can be completed by covering the visible portions of the frame. You can cut two sheets of ¼-inch plywood to the dimensions of the frame to make a very sturdy and permanent cover. Add a single screw at the middle of the top and another at the middle of the bottom. They can be easily removed for repairs or visible demonstrations of the operation.

An alternative material for covering can be heavy-stock colored paper. Cut out the needed size and staple the paper over the openings.

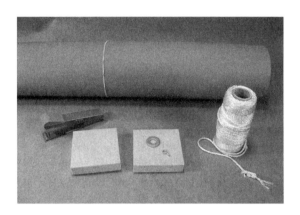

Cardboard Box

Materials

- 2 blocks of wood, 3 in. × 3 in.

- 1 small eyehook

- piece of heavy stock paper 13 in. × 15 in.

- 1 coil of string

- steel washer

This mystery box is quite a bit easier to build than the first one; however, its movement is limited to twice the length of the inside of the box.

Directions

1. Start the construction of this box by cutting the top and bottom plates. They should measure approximately 3 inches square.

2. The wooden block that will be the top plate needs a $^3/_{16}$-inch hole drilled through its center. An easy way to locate the center of this block is to draw diagonal lines from opposing corners.

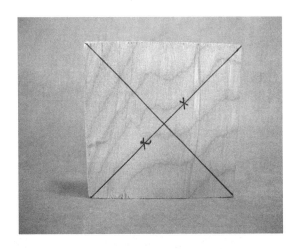

3. The wooden block that will serve as the bottom plate must have a $3/16$-inch drilled hole and an eyehook screw attached to it. To locate the positions for the hole and the hook, first locate the center of this block. Draw diagonal lines from opposing corners. The intersection of the two lines is the center. Measure 1 inch to the left of the center on one of the lines and mark the spot. Drill a $3/16$ inch hole at this position. Measure 1 inch to the right of the center on the same line and mark the spot. Use a sharp object to make an indentation at this position. This is where the eyehook will be screwed in.

4. After drilling the holes, sand the blocks smooth and paint with 1 or 2 coats of varnish.

5. After the varnish is dry, screw the small eyehook into the bottom plate at the indentation made in step 3.

   It is now time to assemble the box.

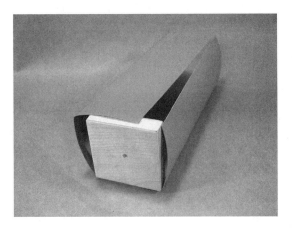

6. The heavy stock paper will form the sides of the box. Measure 3-inch marks on the top and bottom edges of the 13-inch side of the paper. Fold the paper every 3 inches to form the wall of the box. The additional 1 inch of heavy stock paper can be folded to overlap the first wall to completely seal the box.

7. Use a stapler to fasten the paper to 3 of 4 of the sides of the blocks. The eyehook should be on the inside of the box.

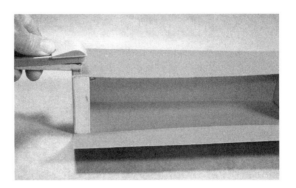

8. Cut a 3-foot length of string and tie one end of the string to the washer. Thread the other end though the center hole in the top plate. Tie a loop onto the end of the string that is outside the box. This will be used to attach the box to some type of hook for hanging.

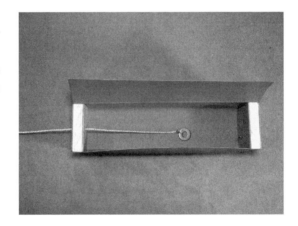

9. Cut a 4-foot length of string and thread it through the center hole in the bottom of the box. The string is then threaded though the washer and then back down to the eyehook. Tie the end of the string to the eyehook.

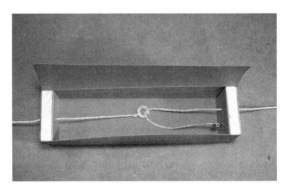

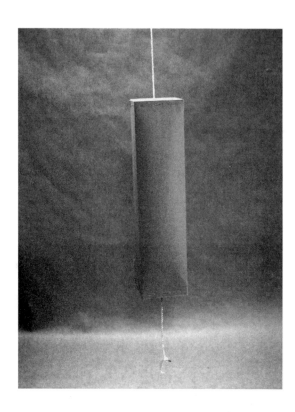

10. Overlap and then staple the last edge of the paper to the top and bottom plates. Then tape the edge of the overlapped side to completely seal the box closed.

Hang the box by the top string and gently pull on the bottom string. The box should go up as the bottom string is pulled down.

Instructional Information

Overview

Blowing up a balloon inside a bottle is difficult if there is no place for the air to be displaced. Once a balloon is blown up inside the bottle, the balloon remains blown up even with the mouth of the balloon wide open. This project is a handy way to recycle a few soda bottles or juice containers and at the same time investigate air pressure and fluids displacement.

Student Skills

Application. Students should be able to identify other situations in which air pressure is added to closed containers such as tires, an air mattress, or a basketball.
Measurements. Students can try using an air pump or pressure gauge and measure the amount of force exerted by the air inside a tire or ball.
Communication. Students can express their understanding to others through drawings and written explanations.

Related Concepts or Processes

Air pressure	Forces
Compression	Gases
Equilibrium	Vacuum
Closed system	Pressure differential

Prior Knowledge

This demonstration can be used for elementary students if they have a basis of understanding for some simple concepts about matter. To start, students need to know that matter can be found as solids, liquids, and gases. All matter can be changed into any of these three states by adding or removing energy. Gases are particles of matter in constant motion. Gas pressure is the result of particles bouncing off any surface with which they come into contact. Gas pressure can increase or decrease by changing a few variables.

Predemonstration Discussion

Because students already have some ideas about air pressure, a balloon can be a very useful tool for reviewing some of these concepts.

Students can make quick drawings to model what they believe is expressed in the questions that are presented. For example, they can draw a model of the air particles inside and outside a deflated balloon.

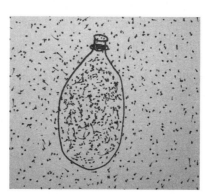

After blowing some air into the balloon, ask students to make another drawing to represent a model of how they think the air and balloon have been changed. The picture represents one student's idea. She is showing that the particles inside the balloon are denser than outside the balloon. She was able to express in her writing that the stretched balloon presses the particles closer together. The pressure inside must be greater than outside of the balloon.

Some suggested questions before showing the bottle can include the following:
- Do you think that air pressure is the same throughout this room?
- Why would air pressure balance itself throughout a room?
- What are some factors that can influence that amount of air pressure?
- If we have an empty balloon and its mouth is open, will there be any difference between the pressure inside and outside?
- If we blow up the balloon, what happens inside in terms of air particles?
- If we squeeze the balloon in our hands, what effect does this have on the volume?
- If we change the volume of the balloon, what effect does this have on the particles?
- Why is air added to a soccer ball?

Suggestions for Presentation

Your students can have fun trying the bottle for themselves. Have several extra balloons available. Before adding the balloon to the top of the jar, discuss what is inside. Next fit a balloon into the jar and stretch the mouth over the mouth of the bottle. Screw the soda bottle cap into place to make the bottle airtight. Then ask a student to try to blow up the balloon inside of the jar. Discussion should follow on why this cannot be done. By this time, most students will have noticed the added soda bottle cap. Usually some suggest trying it again without the cap. If the cap is taken off the bottle, the balloon can then be blown up inside. With the balloon blown up, quickly screw the cap back on. The balloon will remain blown up inside the bottle.

It is unusual that a balloon is blown up due to a decrease in pressure on the outside rather than through the normal method of increased pressure on the inside. Students can look through the opening of the mouth and see down into the center of the balloon.

Interactive questions during the presentation could include the following:

- What is inside the jar?
- Is anything truly empty?
- After a balloon is pushed into the jar and then stretched across the mouth, is there still air inside?
- Why is it impossible to blow up the balloon inside the jar?
- Why does removing the little cap allow us to blow up the balloon?
- Why does the balloon stay inflated if the cap is screwed back on?
- What would happen if we unscrew the little cap?
- What is a method for blowing up the balloon inside the bottle without actually touching it?

Postdemonstration Activities and Discussion

- Write and discuss what would happen to the balloon if this demonstration sits for one or two days.
- What would be the results if we run hot water over the bottle?
- What would happen if we put the device in the freezer for a few minutes? Try it and then discuss the results.
- What would happen if water is added to the inside of the balloon and then the small cap is removed?
- What would happen if water is added to the inside of the balloon and then the device is allowed to sit for a few days?
- You can construct more than one bottle to show variations in demonstrations.

Try using a long balloon inside the soda bottle instead of a round balloon. If the round balloon is blown up inside the soda bottle, the bottle will deform after you stop blowing and the small cap is screwed into place.

You can ask students why the round balloon deforms the bottle while the long balloon does not.

- Which balloon creates a greater pressure change in the space between the balloon and the bottle?
- What size balloon creates more pressure inside, large or small? Hint: When is it hardest to blow up a balloon, when it is small or as it gets bigger?

- Have students draw models to explain the results of the suggested changes to the bottle. The picture represents one student's idea. She is suggesting that the air pressure is decreased inside the bottle but not inside the balloon.

196

- Demonstrate the similarities of adding air to other objects such as a soccer ball or a bike tire. A pump with a gauge can help with a discussion on how pressure is measured.
- Have students research the mechanics of the lungs. How do our lungs work? If we want to pull air into our lungs, what does the body do to the lung? What happens when we exhale?
- Have students make a list of as many objects as possible that have air added to increase the pressure.

Discussion of Results

The amount of pressure is the result of several factors. One factor that pressure depends on is the number of available particles in the gas. Pressure also depends on how frequently and how hard the particles are hitting a surface; this is identified as its kinetic energy. For a given amount of a gas, the volume or size of the container determines or influences the amount of pressure inside. When the amount of gas remains constant and the volume of available space increases, the spacing between the particles increases and the pressure decreases. Decreasing the size of the container has the opposite effect, causing an increase in pressure. Air is a combination of several gases. It exerts pressure against every surface that it touches. Typically, air can exert about 14.7 pounds per square inch of pressure on every surface.

This experiment demonstrates air pressure within a container. As long as air can move into the opening of a container, the pressure will be the same on the inside and outside. Sealing the mouth of the bottle creates a closed container. When a person tries to blow up a balloon inside the container, he or she is making the available space smaller inside the jar. As the space becomes smaller, the particles are pushed closer together, causing them to collide more frequently and increasing the pressure. The balloon will inflate only a small amount because a person's lungs are not strong enough to compress the air much further.

Next, remove the little soda cap and blow up the balloon inside the bottle. Some of the air particles are pushed out of the soda bottle mouth as the balloon inflates. When the soda cap is placed back on, the balloon stays inflated. The reason is that air is unable to return back into this region. As the balloon tries to deflate, it causes an increase in the volume of space between the balloon and the bottle. As the volume increases, the air pressure drops in this region. Without a passage for the air to get past the balloon into the inner part of the bottle, the balloon membrane will remain stretched. Air from outside the bottle is pushing to get into the area of lower pressure inside the bottle.

One postdemonstration has a student blow up the balloon inside the bottle. The condition is that he or she is not allowed to blow into the balloon. The trick to accomplishing this feat is "sucking" on the soda bottle mouth. By doing so, a person decreases the number of air particles in the region, thus lowering the air pressure. Air pressure outside of the bottle inflates the balloon by trying to push into the region. The air is simply trying to equalize itself on both sides of the balloon membrane.

If a 2-liter bottle device is constructed, you can use a long balloon inside a 2-liter soda bottle to keep it from deforming when attempting the first demonstration. However, a long balloon can also deform the bottle if the balloon is not inflated to its full size.

When a round balloon is used inside a soda bottle, it exerts a greater pressure and causes the bottle walls to collapse. Why does this happen? A long balloon conforms to the shape of the soda bottle much better than a round balloon. It can be blown up more completely and forms a larger size balloon inside the bottle. The amount of pressure exerted by the balloon surface is greater in smaller balloons than in larger balloons. This is exhibited when someone is trying to blow up a balloon. Notice that blowing up a balloon is hard when the balloon is very small but gets easier as the balloon gets larger. Pressure is inversely proportional to the radius of the balloon size, so a small balloon collapses or deforms the bottle wall while a larger balloon does not.

Additional Activities

Many demonstrations show the effects of air pressure against a surface. You can make a simple, easy device from a 10 by 12 inch sheet of rubber, a ½-inch dowel, a wood screw, and a 1-inch fender washer.

The screw and washer are on the bottom side of the rubber sheet. The screw is anchored up into the dowel.

As the rubber sheet is pulled upward, a small space is formed right below the dowel. Since there is no air in this space, it is a vacuum. Outside air is pressing to get into this space. As the air is pressing against the rubber, it holds the table surface and the rubber sheet together.

Set the rubber sheet down against the surface of a desk or table. When someone tries to lift the rubber and dowel upward, he or she will lift the table also.

Directions for Assembly

Materials

- 1 plastic bottle, size depends on preference—2 qt., 1 gal., or 2 L
- 1 plastic soda bottle and cap
- 1 large latex balloon
- silicone glue
- WD-40

Juice bottles are more suitable than the 2 L soda bottle. The juice bottles are made with a heavier gauge plastic and do not deform like the soda bottles.

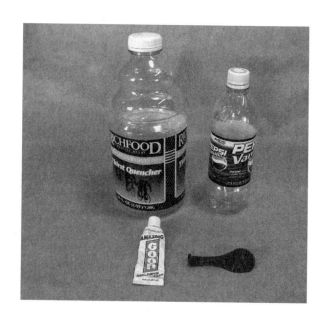

Directions

1. To start, thoroughly clean out both bottles. Remove the label from the 2-quart juice bottle. To do so, blow air from a hair dryer over the outside of the bottle to loosen the glue and then slowly peel the label off. You can remove the excess glue on the bottle by rubbing it with a solvent or WD-40 lubricant.

2. Use a saw to cut off the top of the soda bottle. Keep a ¼-inch portion of the bottleneck right below the grip ring for gluing this section into the quart bottle.

3. The cut edge of the soda bottle must be smooth; otherwise it will puncture the balloon if the two come in contact. Use sandpaper to smooth the edge of the cut soda bottle top.

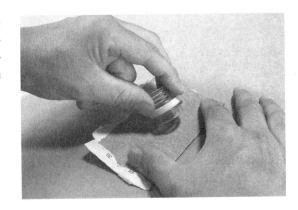

4. Position the soda bottle cap toward the bottom of the bottle, in an area where the bottle is flattened out if possible. Use a pen to trace around the soda bottleneck on to the quart juice bottle.

   The next step is to somehow cut out the area traced onto the bottle. Drilling through the plastic often results in splitting the edges rendering it useless.

If You Build It, They Will Learn

5. The best method of cutting out the correct size hole is to heat a small screwdriver over a stove burner and melt the circumference of the circle. When pushing through the plastic, a sawing action is helpful. Reheat the screwdriver as necessary.

   Check the size of the hole by trying to insert the bottom lip of the soda bottle into this newly cut hole. It should be a snug fit.

6. Firmly glue the soda bottle cap to the plastic bottle. Start by applying a generous bead of glue around the perimeter of the hole.

7. Apply glue also to the bottom edge of the soda bottle lip. Insert the lip into the hole made into the bottle.

202

8. With the soda bottle top in place, apply more glue around the junction if needed.

9. Give the glue a few days to dry. The final procedure is to push a large balloon into the mouth of the bottle. Then stretch the opening of the balloon over the mouth of the bottle and fold it downward to keep it in place.

Caution: Do not twist the bottle cap on too tightly or it may break the glued seal between the bottle and the bottle top.

The 1-liter and 2-liter soda bottles, the 1-gallon juice bottle, and a 2-quart juice bottle are shown ready to go.

The 2-liter soda bottle walls are not as structurally strong as the juice containers. If you have used a soda bottle, use long balloons instead of round balloons. The long balloons will fit better in the bottle, and they do not deform the bottle when the balloons are left inflated inside the bottle.

Instructional Information

Which Surface is the Coldest?
Feel them and see

Overview

The body's senses may not always be accurate judges of its surroundings. In this case, a person's hand compares the relative temperature of three surfaces on the device. The board prompts students to investigate by asking them to determine which surface is coldest. After placing a hand on each of the three surfaces for a few moments, a student usually finds the metal surface feels coldest. In reality, all three surfaces begin at room temperature; they feel cold, warm, and hot due to their different capacities to conduct heat away from the hand.

Student Skills

Observation. This device requires students to make observations using the sense of touch. The observation can be misleading, allowing students to form misconceptions. It is important to follow up with additional activities and explanations that will clarify students' understanding.

Application. Students can use the concept of conductors and insulators and apply it to common practices for retaining energy or transferring energy in common household items and practices.

Conclusion. Students should recognize that thermal energy can transfer from one surface to another. The rate of transfer can depend on several factors, such as the material used, the amount used, the shape, and the airflow around it. Students should be able to determine what some common characteristics of insulators and conductors are.

Related Concepts or Processes

Insulators
Equilibrium
Conduction

Temperature
Kinetic theory of matter
Thermal energy

Prior Knowledge

This piece can appeal to a variety of ages, starting with students around fourth grade. Students should have some basic understanding of concepts such as heat and know that it transfers from one area to another. Even if this age group has not been introduced to the concept of specific heat, they are likely to have an intuitive understanding that some materials are better at retaining heat than others. Students also should have an understanding that some materials are used to slow down the loss of heat and that these types of material are identified as insulators.

Predemonstration Discussion

- What is meant by *hot* and *cold*?
- What are ways of measuring thermal energy?
- What are some characteristics of materials that are good at blocking the loss of heat?
- Why are coats needed in the winter?

Suggestions for Presentation

The set-up and use of this board can fit into the classroom in a variety of ways. The concepts can vary from the study of thermal energy and conductivity to a biological demonstration of the body's senses.

How the board is used can also vary. A common method is to read the words on the base and pass it around for students to try for themselves. The metal may heat up after a few hands have been on it, so try to give it time to cool off after a few tests. Or you can leave this device out for several days for students to test for themselves—they will usually take the first opportunity to do so. They will also seek to confirm their opinions by asking questions, opening several avenues for further studies.

Have students feel each of the surfaces with the palm of the hand for about 10 to 15 seconds. The metal surface will feel cool to the touch, the wood will feel warm, and the foam surface will feel even warmer. If the hand is pressed against the foam surface long enough, it feels like it has been heated.

Interactive questions for discussion could include the following:
- What is the temperature of the room?
- If an object is sitting in this room, what should be its temperature?
- Is there any hidden heat source within the device?
- What is a person's body temperature?
- What do you think happens when a warm object is pressed against a cooler object?

Placing an ice cube on each surface can also demonstrate the differences in the conductivity of the three materials.

Ask students to make predictions before the demonstration is tried. Will the surface that feels the warmest melt the ice faster?

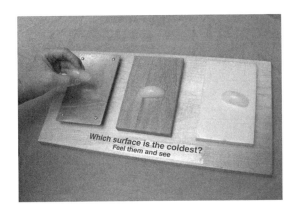

After observing the results of the ice on the demonstration piece, additional materials can be tested in the same manner. Use small ice cubes and place them onto the surface of available samples that are found around the home. Try to use the small size ice cube and limit the amount of time that it is held in the fingers. Some examples of materials and objects to try include the following:
- different types of plastics
- different types of metals
- different sizes and thicknesses of plastic and metal plates.
- the bottoms of different-sized pots and pans
- ceramic cups
- glass cups
- paper cups
- foam cups
- tin cans
- metal plates laying flat against a surface or being held away from other surfaces
- small ice cube held in the hand

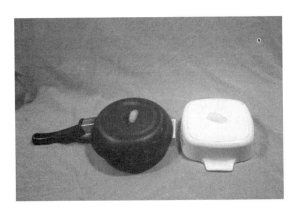

The picture at the bottom of p. 207 shows a black metal pan and a white ceramic bowl. The two variables should stimulate questions about which might have the greater effect on the ice. You can use this demonstration as a lead-in to student-designed experiments for testing materials.

Interactive questions for discussion could include the following:
- Rank the materials according to which will melt the ice cube, fastest to slowest.
- List some reasons for your choices.
- Black pan or white ceramic—which variable is causing the ice to melt faster?
- How might these variables be tested?
- What types of surfaces would you want to conduct heat very quickly?
- What are some surfaces that you would not want to conduct heat?

Postdemonstration Activities and Discussion

Ideas for writing prompts or activities could include the following:
- How might this experiment be different in very hot temperatures?
- Why is the body not always a good judge of temperature?
- Why is it not a good idea to have walls made only of metal?
- Have students verify the temperature of the different surfaces using a thermometer.
- The type of material and the thickness determine the rate of energy loss.
Design experiments that could be used to test the insulating properties of various materials.

Discussion of Results

The skin of the hand can detect differences between the body's temperature and temperatures outside of the body through nerve endings located in the skin. Touch any surface that is at a lower temperature than body temperature, and initially it will feel cool to the touch. What happens is that, as you press against an object, some of the heat from your hand will transfer to the object that you are touching. This cools the skin down and triggers the nerve endings in the skin to tell you that the surface is cool to cold, depending on how much heat is lost from the hand.

If no one were touching the surfaces, the temperature on all three materials would be the same, around 70 degrees Fahrenheit or 23 degrees Celsius. The surfaces will feel like they are at different temperatures because the surfaces carry away different amounts of heat. The more heat that is carried away, the colder the surface seems to be.

The ability to carry heat through a surface is called conduction. The metal on the board is aluminum, which is able to carry away the most heat from the surface of the hand. Therefore, it feels as if it is the coldest surface. The wood is a poor conductor of heat, and, as your hand touches it, less heat is carried away from the hand than when your hand touches the metal, so this surface feels as if it is warmer.

The expanded foam is a very poor conductor of heat. Materials such as these are called insulators. As your hand presses against this surface, very little heat is carried away. The surface warms up to the same temperature as your hand very quickly, and then very little additional heat is lost from the skin. The nerve endings of the hand stay warm, and the body is fooled into thinking that this surface is warmer than the others.

The ice, left on the surfaces for 1 minute, will show a dramatic difference in the amount melted by the aluminum plate compared to the amount melted by the wood and the foam blocks. Because the aluminum plate is such a good conductor, more thermal energy is transferred from the plate into the ice. Some of this energy is coming from the metal itself. The aluminum is also capable of conducting more thermal energy from the air surrounding it than the other materials. This thermal energy is causing the ice to melt. Since the ice is absorbing thermal energy from the metal plate, the plate's temperature will be lowered by about 30 to 40 degrees Fahrenheit. Placing a thermometer against the surface can show this.

After 2 minutes, the ice cube on the aluminum plate will be completely melted. The ice on the wood may show a small amount of melting, while the cube on the foam will be unchanged.

To reinforce the idea of conductors and insulators, have students touch each plate at various locations. The metal plate is very cold all over while the wood will feel cold only directly beneath where the ice was sitting. The foam block does not feel cold anyplace except for where the ice cube was sitting, but, because it is a better insulator, it will not feel as cold as the wood.

For ice to melt, it must absorb energy. The ice that sits on the aluminum absorbs energy from the entire plate, which is why the whole plate feels very cold. The aluminum plate gives up energy to the ice but at the same time is absorbing thermal energy from the air. This is why it melts so quickly. A larger aluminum plate would melt the ice even faster. If most of the aluminum plate is covered with masking tape, the rate of melting will decrease because the energy from the air cannot be absorbed as readily.

The insulating properties of the wood and the foam allow very little energy to transfer into the ice from either of these two materials. Because they are good insulators, they will not absorb thermal energy from the air and transfer it into the ice. Therefore, almost all of the energy that will eventually melt the ice must come from the heated air in the room itself.

Interactive questions for discussion could include the following:
• Why is the metal plate so cold?
• Will the metal plate eventually warm up? Why?
• If we let the ice cubes remain on the wood and the foam block, what will happen to them eventually?
• Where will the energy come from to melt the ice?

Additional Activities

Students can investigate some methods used to intentionally increase or decrease the warming or cooling rates of containers. This experiment can be done in two parts. Each part is tested by filling empty soda cans with 150 ml of hot tap water. Students measure the temperature drop every 20 seconds for 20 minutes.

Part one is intended to determine ways of cooling a can and contents as quickly as possible. Give students an assignment to design or alter a soda can, using aluminum foil and tape, to make it cool off the 150 ml of hot water faster than an unaltered can.

The example shows a student-designed "radiator soda can." It has several strips of aluminum foil loops taped to it to act as "cooling fins."

For part two, have students design methods to slow the loss of heat from a soda can. Once again, students fill the can with hot water and measure the temperature every 20 seconds for 20 minutes. In this case, students can use various insulating materials to retain the thermal energy as long as possible. Students can compare insulating materials such as paper, masking tape, foam bits, blow-in insulation, types of cloth, jackets, socks, shirts, hats, and soda can holders specifically made to keep soda cans cool.

After collecting data, students can graph their results and draw conclusions from their findings.

Directions for Assembly

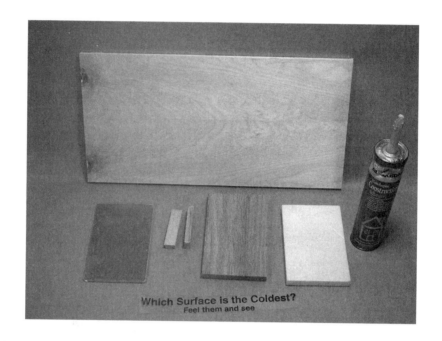

Which Surface is the Coldest?
Feel them and see

Materials

- 1 piece of plywood, 9 in. × 18 in.
- 1 piece of solid wood, 4 in. × 6 in.
- 1 piece of foam insulation, 4 in. × 6 in.
- 1 piece of sheet metal, aluminum or steel, 4 in. × 6 in.
- 1 transparency, 8.5 in. × 11 in.
- 2 pieces of wood, ¼-in. thick, 1 in. × 4 in.
- glue

The most difficult job for this piece may be locating a suitable metal plate. Several different types and thicknesses of metal would be suitable and may be available at a local metal fabrication shop. A check in the yellow pages might yield a supplier.

Directions

1. Cut a piece of plywood to the approximate dimensions of 9 by 18 inches. Sand the edges and surface smooth in preparation for varnishing. Cut the foam, wood block, and the sheet metal to 4 by 6 inch size. If the available metal plate is another dimension, cut the wood and foam to match it. The wood and metal plate should be smooth and free of sharp edges. Print the words "Which Surface Is the Coldest? Feel them and See" onto paper or a transparency using a computer and printer. Cut the words all in one strip of material rather than individually. To attach the strip, paint the surface of plywood board with a coat of varnish and then press the printed paper or transparency into the wet surface. Let dry and apply a second coat of varnish.

2. Place the foam, wood, and metal in position on the plywood. They should be evenly spaced and all located the same height from the top. Use a pencil to mark the positions on the board. Apply a sufficient amount of glue onto the foam, and then press the foam firmly into place according to the penciled marks. Repeat this procedure for the wood block.

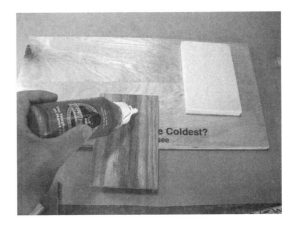

3. Do not glue the metal directly to the plywood surface. It should be mounted above the surface of the plywood using 2 small pieces of wood as spacers. Glue the small pieces of wood to the plywood surface, and then glue the metal to these two supports.

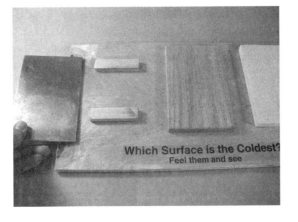

4. A third coat of varnish applied over the transparency words will help protect them. Use 1 coat of varnish on the section of wood that is touched to keep it from absorbing water from the melted ice.

The completed project.

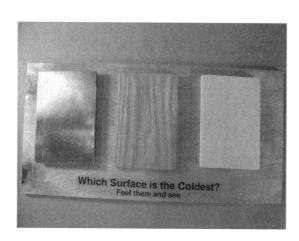

Which Surface is the Coldest?
Feel them and see

Instructional Information

Overview

Around a hole on top of a can or on the side of a cardboard box the words "What color is inside?" appear. The outside of each container is multi-colored, indicating that any of a number of colors could be inside. If you look through the hole, it appears that the inside is painted black. You can challenge students to determine what color is inside without prying off the lid or opening the box. When you reveal what color is inside, students gain insight into the nature of our perception of light, color, and what is needed for our eyes to see. The informational instruction is written for the can, although a box could be used instead.

Student Skills

Draw a Conclusion. Students should conclude that adequate amounts of light are needed for vision. If you try additional activities, they should take into account that detecting color requires more light than detecting black and white.

Trial and Error. Students can attempt several simple strategies to determine the color inside the can.

Research. Students can search for additional information on how light is reflected and refracted by a lens. They can also learn how light is captured by the eye.

Communication. Students can express their understanding of the concepts through the use of drawings and written explanations.

Related Concepts or Processes

Light
Color
Reflection

Prior Knowledge

This demonstration is applicable to a wide range of students, starting as early as those in fourth grade. What makes this piece particularly useful is that it can address misconceptions that students have about light. Students should have been introduced to some basic concepts of light. They should know that light is energy and is needed for us to see. They may know that light rays bounce off of objects and that our eyes receive some of this reflected light.

Predemonstration Discussion

Many students have a common misconception about light. Middle-school students often think they can see without a light source. Part of this misconception may come from watching movies in which people in dark areas or caves are still able to see. The students believe that, if they were put in a room with no light, they would be able to see after their eyes adjusted to the darkness and insist they would be able to tell the difference between a light object and a dark object.

Questions for discussion before demonstrating the can include the following:
- What is the difference between light and dark?
- How is a person able to see?
- Is light needed to see an object?
- What would happen if you were placed in a room without any light?
- Would you eventually be able to see in a cave?
- Are you able to see colors at nighttime?

Suggestions for Presentation

This piece can be presented to students as part of a lecture/discussion, or it can be set out for students to investigate on their own.

The paint can lid should be pressed down tight enough that students cannot pull it off. If the box is used instead of the paint can, use some clear plastic tape to seal the flaps so that it cannot be opened. All students should have the opportunity to try and peer into the container. Some will try to hold it at various angles near a bright light or in sunshine to get light inside.

216

After all students have had the opportunity to try and see into the can, ask them to make predictions about the color inside. After discussion, try the additional suggested activities or use a screwdriver to gently pry off the lid and reveal the contents.

Interactive questions to ask about the can include the following:
• What color do you see when you look into the hole in the can?
• What color do you think is inside?
• Why did you pick that color?
• What color do you think would be easiest to see?
• Why can't we see the inside of the can?
• What does this tell us about what is needed for us to see color?
• Can you think of any ways to determine what color is inside?
• Why can we now tell what color is inside when the lid is off?
• Is black a color?

Postdemonstration Activities and Discussion

Have students write an explanation about the sequence of requirements that allow one to see an object.

Colored blocks can be compared in different intensities of light until the color no longer can be distinguished.

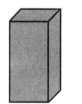

At home, students can identify the color of several objects and then take them to a darkened room or a closet. They should adjust the light level until the color is no longer distinguishable. They can then write a detailed review describing their findings.

Ask them to consider if some items are easier than others to distinguish in low light.

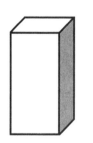

If a darkroom is available, give students the opportunity to test their ability to see in pitch darkness. This can also be an assignment that students could try at home. Have students try to tell the difference black blocks and white blocks.

Show a circle of heavy-stock white paper and a circle of heavy-stock black paper with holes in them that are the same diameter as the hole in the can. When you hold the black paper against the white, it appears very black.

Hold the black paper against the can and match up the hole in the paper with the hole in the can. The black paper will look gray when seen against the blackness of the hole.

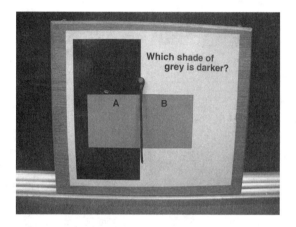

You can show the contrast of black and white with another device to put on display for students to investigate.

From a distance, it appears there are two shades of gray on a sheet of paper. The apparently lighter shade of gray is set against a black background. The apparently darker shade of gray is set against a white background.

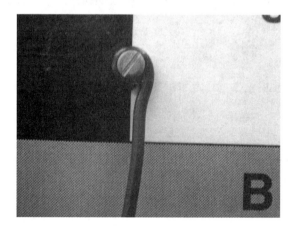

Between the two gray blocks is a piece of black wire bent around a screw in the wood. The wire is a piece of 12-gauge common household wire with black plastic insulation.

The wire can be pushed up out of the way to reveal that the blocks are both the same.

The paper is a simple setup made on a computer and then printed. Laminate it so that it will stand up better to students' touching it.

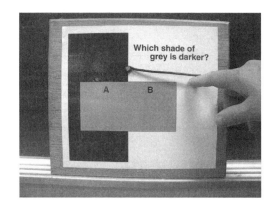

Discussion of Results

As noted, the idea that our eyes can adjust to seeing in absolute darkness is one of the misconceptions many students carry with them into middle school and beyond. This demonstration of trying to peer into a darkened can should correct that misconception.

Our eyes function by catching a small amount of light as it is reflected off various surfaces and colors. For example, if you are reading this text, the page must be illuminated by some light source. Some of the light not absorbed by the page is reflected and travels to the eye where it is turned into electric impulses carried to the brain. The black ink in the written text will absorb light rather than reflect it, so the light that strikes the letters and words on these pages does not reach the eye.

A person can see shapes and shades of black and white long after there is so little light that he or she can no longer distinguish color. The human eye uses different receptors and is more sensitive to achromatic contrast (black and white) than it is to chromatic contrast (color). Contrast is the perceived difference between two adjacent colors. Because white and black are not really colors, they are said to represent achromatic contrast. Black and white also represent the highest level of contrast. Complementary colors found on a color wheel would represent the highest amount of chromatic contrast, but the contrast is not nearly as great as between black and white. This is why text is usually written with black words on a white background (white words written on black background uses much more ink).

The retina of the human eyes contains more than one hundred million cones and rods capable of sending messages to the brain. To help us cope with receiving so much information, the brain must condense some of this information to the million neurons that carry the messages it receives. One way they do lies in the way we perceive areas of high contrast. As our eyes look at contrasting areas of light and dark, such as black and white, regions of the retina that are stimulated by looking at light areas tend to dampen nearby contrasting dark areas seen in the retina. This means the dark areas will tend to look darker. It also means that light areas near the dark regions will appear to seem lighter. This is demonstrated by the white and black round discs. The dark card appears black next to the white but seems gray compared to the black region in the hole of the can. This action is called lateral inhibition. This is also demonstrated by the gray samples surrounded by the light or the dark backgrounds. The gray sample surrounded by the black background appears to be a lighter shade than the gray sample surrounded by the white. The wire acts as a boundary that allows the brain to be fooled into separating the gray into two distinct regions and shades. When the wire is lifted, the boundary is removed and the eye sees the gray as all the same shade.

When there is enough light to see color, our eyes perceive blue, red, green, and about 10 million other shades of color. The human eye distinguishes objects based on the wavelength of the light reflected or emitted by the object. There is some conjecture about the process, but the brain must be able to identify the various hues according to a commonly held language that we use to describe each shade. An apple may be red because it absorbs all the frequencies of light shining on it other than those frequencies we perceive and identify as red, which are reflected by the apple.

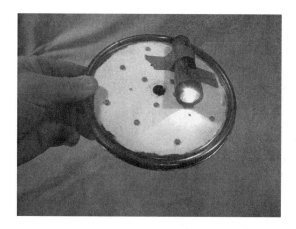

Additional Activities

The color inside the can appears to be black because a sufficient amount of visible light cannot get inside and reflect out again so that the actual color can be seen. The hole in the lid is large enough to allow the viewer to see the color inside, if there were a light source on the other side. You can tape a small flashlight inside the can and then seal the container. When the flashlight is lit, it is very easy to see the color and, if you've added words at the bottom, even to read those words.

You can alter the perceived color inside the illuminated can by covering the flashlight with a colored filter. Make a second lid for the container that has a hole large enough to allow a small flashlight to illuminate the inside.

Cover the flashlight with cellophane tape different in color than the color inside the can. You can also cover it with clear plastic tape painted with a colored marker. Insert the light back into the opening of the can lid. Also try taping different-colored paper to the bottom of the can to see how the added colors of light will alter perception of the paper color.

Directions for Assembly

> **Paint Can Materials**
>
> - several colors of spray paint
> - white paint, in spray can or liquid form
> - 1 empty gallon-size paint can in good condition
> - 1 piece of pine wood, $5 \times 5 \times \frac{3}{4}$ in.
> - 8 wood screws, $\frac{3}{4}$ in. long
> - 1 clear sheet of plastic, $8\frac{1}{2} \times 11$ in.

Directions

1. Clean out the 1-gallon paint can, and wire brush all surfaces to remove loose bits. An ideal method is to use a round wire-brush attachment mounted on an electric drill.

   After a thorough cleaning, paint the inside of the can with 1 or 2 coats of white paint. Tape the ridges at the top of the can to keep it from being painted.

2. The outside of the can should be painted with several colors to hide the true color of the inside of the can. The more colors available, the better.

SAFETY NOTE

For the next series of instructions, the following safety equipment is strongly recommended:

• Goggles for eye protection. NSTA recommends that you use safety goggles that conform to the ANSI Z87.1 standard and that provide both impact and chemical-splash protection for all science laboratory work.

• Dust mask to guard against breathing in airborne sawdust.

• Gloves whenever power tools are used.

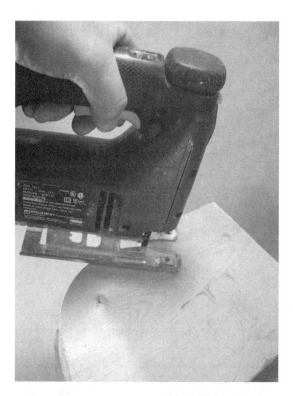

3. The paint can lid must have material added to block some of the light that could enter the can. Without the wood, the demonstration still works if the size of the hole is reduced to ¼-inch diameter. Use a compass to draw a 4-inch circle on the scrap of wood. Then use a wood saw to cut out the circle.

4. The hole in the center of the disc should be drilled with a ⅜-inch bit. Place the disc on a scrap piece of wood to protect the table surface. Sand the wood and apply 1 coat of varnish to the wood.

5. The 4-inch wood disc is measured to fit inside the ridges that circle the top of the can lid. It can be made smaller, but it also gives ample room for the words to be added to the wood surface.

6. Turn the lid and wood disc over and drill 8 small ½-inch deep pilot holes through the can lid into the wood disc. Five of the holes should be spaced evenly around the outside perimeter of the lid; the 3 remaining holes should be spaced evenly around the center. The number and spacing of the screws keep the lid from flexing as it is pushed on or pried off of the can.

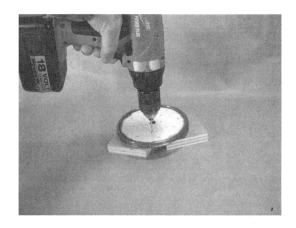

7. Screw the wood screws through the lid into the wood to hold the lid and disc together.

8. With the disk firmly attached to the lid, use the ⅜-inch drill bit to drill a hole though the metal portion of the wood-and-lid combination. Paint the inside wall of the drilled hole with a flat black paint to help minimize light passing into the can.

9. Print the words "What color is inside?" and "Science is cool" on paper using a computer and printer. You can print the words on a transparent plastic sheet instead of paper.

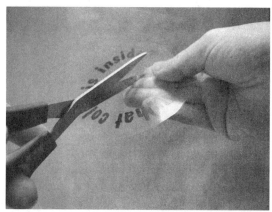

10. Use scissors to cut around the words, keeping an extra ½-inch of material beyond the printing. Cut a 2-inch circle from the center of the material. This will leave the hole unobstructed.

11. To attach the paper or plastic to the disk, paint the wood disk with a second coat of varnish, and, while the varnish is still wet, press the transparency onto the wet surface. Give the varnish plenty of time to dry, especially if words were printed on plastic.

To apply "Science is cool" to the bottom of the can, apply some white paint to the bottom of the can and press the paper or plastic into the wet paint. Allow the varnish to dry before applying a second coat.

12. Place the lid on the top of the can and press it firmly into place. Do not press too hard or the lid will be difficult to get off and may bend in the process. Try peering into the can to determine what color is inside. The inside should look black even though it is painted white.

13. If you want a second lid for the can, cut another round disk from wood to match the size of the metal lid.

14. Then cut two holes into the wood disk. Locate the smaller, ½-inch hole in the center. Cut the larger hole to match the diameter of a small flashlight.

15. If the flashlight does not fit snuggly into the hole in the disk, make it fit by wrapping a few layers of tape around the top section.

16. Attach the wood disk to the metal lid using the ½-inch wood screws.

What Color Is Inside?

17. If the wood bit cannot drill through the metal of the lid, make a large hole by drilling several small holes. You can use pliers to bend back any metal pieces that are in the way of the light.

Cardboard Box
Materials

• several colors of spray paint

• white paint, in spray can or liquid form

• cardboard box

A cardboard box is an easy alternative to a paint can as the container for this demonstration. This particular box measures 8 in. × 8 in. × 12 in. and has overlapping edges that block out all the unwanted light that might come in through the seams. After you get a suitable box, check it to see that the seams do not allow light through.

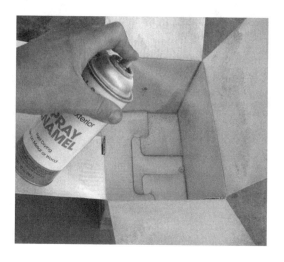

Directions

1. You can seal the seams with masking tape or duct tape if they do not block the light adequately.

2. Paint the inside of the box either with spray paint or with a brush and a can of paint.

3. Paint the exterior of the box with a multitude of colors in the same way as the can is painted.

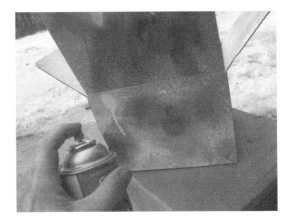

4. Drill a ½-inch hole into the side of the box. Spray white paint around the hole to give it a better contrast to the black of the inside of the box.

Print the words "What color is inside?" around the hole to pique the interest of students.

Instructional Information

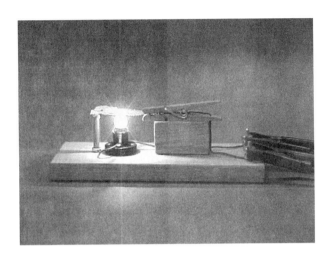

Overview

If a student examines a typical thermostat, he or she will find a thin bar inside that is made from two different metals bonded together in a long narrow strip. When the strip is heated, it will bend into a slightly curved shape. When the strip cools, it will straighten to its original shape. This process is the basis for the action of a thermostat and is widely used to control the temperature of heating or cooling devices such as ovens, toasters, refrigerators, and space heaters.

This device shows how a thermostat works by turning a lightbulb on and off as the thermostat responds to the heat of the bulb. It can use a gum wrapper or a strip made from paper and aluminum foil to act as a thermostat mechanism. It behaves and demonstrates the same principles as a commercially made device, but is much safer, because it does not require high temperatures that are unsafe for young hands.

This device can be made larger using car bulbs or exterior low-voltage lightbulbs and a 12-volt power source. Do not use higher voltage because of the potential for electric shock.

Student Skills

Observation. Students observe the blinking light for a long enough period of time to determine if the blinking occurs at a fairly constant rate.

Application. Students should be able to identify a variety of other appliances or situations that uses a thermostat to control temperature.

Testing Hypothesis. Students can suggest and make changes to the compound bar to determine what factors affect the results.

Communication. Students can demonstrate their understanding through the use of drawings and written explanations.

Related Concepts or Processes

Electrical circuits	Thermal energy
Energy changes	Bimetallic strip or compound bar
Coefficient of expansion	Expansion and contraction of matter

Prior Knowledge

You might find this device useful when discussing electrical circuits and additional ways to control them or in the discussion of thermal expansion and the properties of matter.

In either case, students must have an understanding of some basic science concepts. The first concept is that a complete circuit is needed for electricity to flow. When the circuit is broken, the flow of electricity is interrupted and the device will stop working. The second concept that students must understand is that most matter expands as it is heated and contracts as it cools. Although there are several exceptions, this process holds true for solids, liquids, and gases and may be applicable to both metals and nonmetals.

Predemonstration Discussion

Questions for review might include the following:

*   How do we control the temperature inside such things as ovens, heaters, and refrigerators?
*   After we turn a temperature dial, what happens inside these devices?
*   How does the switch determine if it is hot enough or cold enough?

Use a lightbulb and battery to review how a circuit works. Using two wires, connect a lightbulb to each side of a battery so that the bulb is lit. Next, randomly break the circuit to make the bulb blink on and off and discuss the results. You can ask the following questions:

*   How do circuits work?
*   What happens when an electric circuit is broken? Why?
*   What are the energy changes that occur when the lightbulb is lit?
*   What two energy forms are given off when a lightbulb is lit?

Review thermal energy. Questions you could ask include the following:

*   What happens to matter as it is heated or cooled?

- Does this occur for solids, liquids, and gases?
- What are some examples where this process occurs? (Examples might include hot air balloons, cracks in sidewalks, metal bridges, and thermometers.)

Suggestions for Presentation

This piece can operate for several hours without needing adjustment. Perhaps the best way to demonstrate it is to have it in operation before students enter the classroom. You can then discuss its action after the class lesson.

The movement of the compound bar is very slight and may not be noticeable to students unless they observe the piece closely. On close examination, they will see that the compound bar breaks contact with the brass bolt head and then slowly returns to touch it again.

To show the movement more clearly, hold another handmade compound bar just over another source of heat such as a 100-watt lightbulb or a lit candle.

For this demonstration, you do not need to paint the aluminum foil black. Seeing that the intense heat will cause the strip to bend is easy, but the higher heat may cause the strip to exceed its ability to recover and unbend.

SAFETY NOTE
Because of the hot flame and hot wax, take care when working with a lit candle.

Have students try making their own compound strips using paper labels and aluminum foil so they can observe this process for themselves. An alternative to making the strips would be to have students try using foil-backed gum wrappers—instant compound bars!

Interactive questions during presentation could include the following:
- Why is the bulb lit? What does this tell us about the circuit?
- Why does the bulb go out? What does this tell us about the circuit?
- Why does the bulb come back on again?
- Where might this action be useful?

Gum Wrapper Thermostat

- How might we speed up this process, or how could we slow down this process?
- Would this work if the strip were turned upside down? Why?
- Why is the foil side painted black?

Postdemonstration Suggestions and Discussion

- Have students search and then list as many devices as they can find that may contain a thermostat.
- Have students write in a journal and explain how a thermostat works.
- Have students discuss some variables that might determine how quickly the lightbulb blinks.
- Have students design and investigate these variables to determine the effects that they may have on the blinking rate of the lightbulb.

Possible variables to test include the following:
- straight surface versus a bent surface for the compound bar
- type of paper
- thickness of aluminum foil
- other types of metal foil
- color and type of paint on aluminum side of the strip
- width and/or length of the compound strip
- amperage of the lightbulb
- temperature as compared to distance bent

After learning how this simple thermostat operates, have students design a control mechanism that would allow someone to adjust the thermostat to a higher or lower temperature using dials, a slide bar, or other means.

Discussion of Results

This demonstration shows how a thermostat using a compound strip can control the cycling on and off of various heating or cooling devices such as stoves, household heaters, toasters, blinking lights, clothes dryers, and freezers.

The compound strip is made of two different types of materials—in this case, aluminum and paper. Paper is made from tiny strands of cellulose and does not tend to change in size due to slight changes in heat. The aluminum, on the other hand, expands as it is heated and contracts as it is cooled. These two surfaces are joined together, and, when they are heated, the aluminum expands, but the paper does not.

The strip will bend to allow for the expansion. The material that expands more is on the outside of the curved surface. Obviously, real thermostats would not be made of paper and aluminum, but the principle is the same. Real thermostats use a strip that is made of brass on one side and iron on the other. These are usually referred to as bimetallic, or two-metal, strips. Once again the material with the greater coefficient of thermal expansion (the material that expands more) will be found on the outer side of the curving strip. When cooled, the reverse action would occur. When cooled, the material that expanded more now contracts to a shorter length and now will be found on the inside curved portion of the strip. These bimetallic strips are readily available as an additional demonstration of thermal expansion.

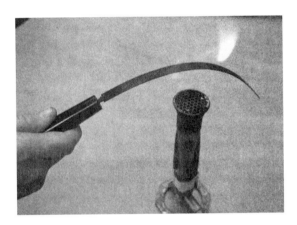
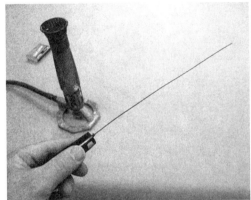

Additional Activities

Bimetallic strips are found in many devices. You may want to ask around and locate old appliances that contain a thermostat so you can disassemble them to retrieve the thermostat. Some appliances use a straight piece of bimetallic strip, while others use a coiled piece.

Try making homemade bimetallic strips of two different types of metal—for example, aluminum and copper. These metals are available as adhesive-backed foil and can be purchased from sources such as craft shops, hardware stores, or hobby shops.

Students can look up the coefficient of expansion for different metals and suggest what two materials may yield the most movement.

Directions for Assembly

Materials

- 1 miniature lightbulb base
- 1 miniature lightbulb 6-V, 300 mA
- 1 brass round head bolt, 10–32 × 2 in.
- 2 steel flat head bolts, 10–32 × 1.5 in.
- 3 10–32 steel nuts
- 2 brass knobs, size 10–32
- 2 small screws, #4 × ½ in.
- 1 piece of aluminum foil
- 3 mailing address labels, 1 in. × 3 in. long
- 1 plastic straw
- 1 piece of wood, 3.5 in. × 8 in.,
- 1 piece of wood, 2 in. × 1¼ in.
- 1 clothespin
- foil chewing gum wrappers

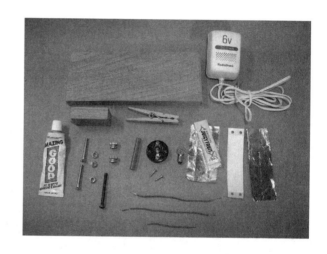

Directions

1. This project begins with the wood base. Cut it to an approximate size of 3½ inches by 8 inches. After cutting the block, sand the edges and surfaces smooth.

    Attach the lightbulb base approximately 2 inches from the right side using the 2 small screws. If the device base is a hardwood such as oak, you will have to drill pilot holes before screwing them in. After the base is secure, screw the lightbulb into the base.

234

2. For this device to work, the height of the compound strip must be about 1 to 2 millimeters directly above the bulb. The height of the strip is determined by the thickness of the clothespin and the block on which it sits. The height of the small block is approximately 1¼ inches. Before attaching the block to the wood base, determine that it is at the correct height by putting the block on the base, and then lay the clothespin on top of the small block. The bottom jaw of the clothespin should be about the same height as the top of the lightbulb. Put a piece of heavy paper into the clothespin to check the height.

3. After checking that the block is cut to the correct height, position the block edge about 1½ inches away from the lightbulb. Use wood glue or epoxy to attach the small block to the base at this position. An alternative method is to use wood screws to attach the block to the base. If using the screw method, drill pilot holes from the underside of the base into the wood block before screwing the wood screws into position. Glue the clothespin onto the top of the small block whose edge is approximately 1 inch away from the center of the lightbulb.

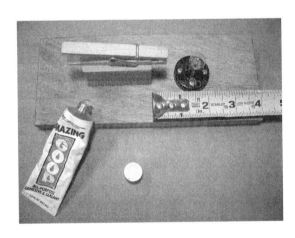

4. On the opposite side of the lightbulb, drill a ⅛-inch hole about 1⅛ inches away from the bulb. Screw the nut onto the brass bolt, and then screw the bolt into this hole. The height of the brass bolt should be about 1 to 2 millimeters higher than the top of the lightbulb. This height can be fine-tuned later.

SAFETY NOTE

The following safety equipment is strongly recommended:

- Goggles for eye protection. NSTA recommends that you use safety goggles that conform to the ANSI Z87.1 standard and that provide both impact and chemical-splash protection for all science laboratory work.
- Dust mask to guard against breathing in airborne sawdust.
- Gloves whenever power tools are used.

5. The 2 steel bolts are used to anchor the power source to the thermostat. They should be positioned in the corners of the wood base. Turn the base over and prop it on some wood scraps. Drill pilot holes through the wooden base.

6. Screw the steel bolts up from the bottom through the drilled holes. The heads of these steel bolts must be flush with the underside surface, or they may scratch the tabletop surface that they sit on. Hand tighten the steel nuts down to the wood. The brass knobs will eventually anchor power source wires to this device. This might be a good time to varnish the wood parts, before the wiring is added. Sand all edges and surface. Signing your name and date to the underside of the base before varnishing is a nice touch.

7. It is now time to cut and attach the wiring for this device. Start by cutting a wire to a length of 1½ inches long; then strip ¼ inch of insulation from each end. Attach one end of this wire to the screw of the light socket. Wrap the other end around the bottom brass bolt. Use the nut to tighten the wire down against the wood base.

8. The second wire needs to be about 5 inches long. Cut this length and then strip ¼ inch of insulation off each end. Attach this wire to the second side of the light socket. Wrap the other end around the bottom of one of the steel bolts. Use a nut to tighten the wire down against the wood base.

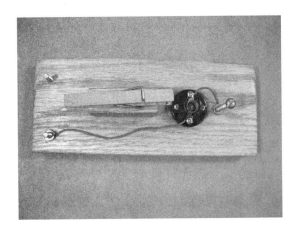

9. The third wire runs from the clothespin to the other steel bolt. Before attaching the wire, drill a small hole in the bottom side of the clothespin for this wire to run through. Next, cut off a 4-inch length of wire and strip ½ inch of insulation off one end. Remove ¼ inch of insulation from the other end of this wire. Push the ½-inch end of bare wire through the spring of the clothespin. When this device is in operation, this wire must make contact with the aluminum foil of the compound strip.

10. This wire starts in the spring of the clothes-pin. The other end of the wire is threaded through the hole in the clothespin and stretched over to the second steel bolt. Wrap the bare end of the wire around the bottom of the second steel bolt and use a nut to tighten the wire down against the wood base. You can now add the brass knobs back onto these bolts to hold the power supply wires in place.

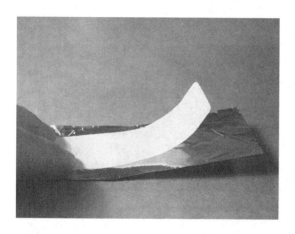

11. Make the compound strips using mailing address labels that are 1 by 3 inches. Peel off the paper backing and apply this label to a smooth piece of aluminum foil. If the aluminum foil is wrinkled, rub it flat with the palm of the hand. Use scissors to cut the excess foil from around the edges of the label. One-inch-wide masking tape can be used instead of the mailing label, but it may not work quite as well.

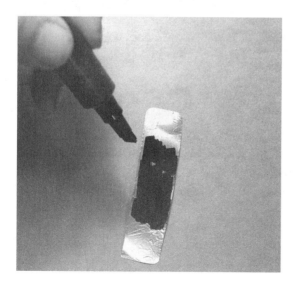

12. Use a black felt-tipped marker to color the center area of the foil. This area will be directly above the lightbulb. The black allows the aluminum to absorb more light energy from the bulb and heat more quickly.

13. Use fine sandpaper to scratch the top of the brass bolt and the wire in the mouth of the clothespin. This allows better contact between the foil and the contact points.

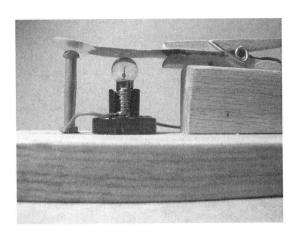

Open the clothespin and slide the compound strip (aluminum side down) in far enough to make contact with the bare wire. The other end of the strip should be resting on the brass bolt. The compound strip should just barely touch or be slightly above the lightbulb. If not, screw the brass bolt up or down until it is in the correct position.

14. Use scissors to cut down the length of a straw and then cut a section just long enough to cover the exposed brass threads on the brass bolt. Slide the straw onto the bolt for a neater appearance.

15. Wrap wire from the power source around the two steel bolts and then hold it in place by tightening the brass nuts down against the steel nuts. A 6-volt power adapter, a 6-volt lantern battery, or some other source of 6-volt DC supply can power this device.

16. When the power source is added to the connections, the bulb should light up. It can take the bulb about 30 seconds to 1 minute to start blinking. When working properly, the bulb should blink on and off in approximately 20- to 30-second cycles.

17. An alternative to the label and foil strip is a foil-backed gum wrapper as the compound strip. Once again, color the foil side black with a marker where it will be exposed to the light source. Use as described in steps 14 and 15. Gum wrapper thermostats tend to be a bit more "finicky" and require more adjustments but still perform satisfactorily.

18. Scratch the points of contact occasionally with a very fine sandpaper to remove tarnish. This includes the area on the foil where it contacts the wire and brass bolt head. The strips may need to be bent down for them to make contact with the brass bolts.

Instructional Information

 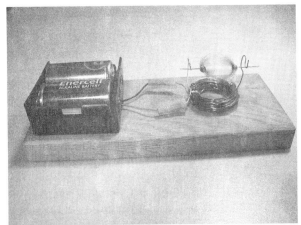

Overview

Using some very simple materials, you can produce an electric motor with which you can demonstrate the principles of magnetism. A variation of the simple motor replaces the usual ceramic magnet with a coil of wire to form an electromagnet. Both pieces are fairly simple to build and can be entertaining as well as instructional.

Student Skills

Design and Construct. Students can build their own motor specifically following the directions given in this book, or they can attempt to improve on this design. This motor is an introduction to how motors work. There are many designs for motors that are more efficient and useful.

Observation. Students can observe the action of the motor turning and manually feel the forces exerted on the coil by holding it in place while it is energized.

Application. Students can expand on the concept of magnetism by identifying other situations in which electromagnets can be used.

Related Concepts or Processes

Electricity	Magnetism
Circuits	Series circuits
Torque	Currents

Prior Knowledge

The simple motor is an engaging activity for students in grades four and higher. Younger students can construct these motors with adult supervision and assistance. For this activity to be appropriate, students should have some basic understanding of electricity and magnetism. They should know that electricity needs a complete circuit to flow. Before building the motor, students also should know that wrapping wire around a D-cell battery to form a coil would increase a magnetic field. They should have some understanding that magnetic fields can attract or repel other magnetic fields. The attraction or repulsion is dependent on the orientation of the magnets. Students viewing the double-coiled motor should understand the operation of the simple motor prior to viewing this additional piece.

Predemonstration Discussion

Before introducing simple motors, you should dedicate some time to a review or some basic instruction about magnet fields and electricity. Here are two activities that every student should experience.

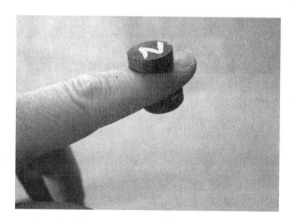

Every student should have the opportunity to discover the attraction and repulsion of permanent magnets. Simple disk magnets are extremely cheap and available from a variety of sources. Try to find magnets that are identified with an *N* and an *S* to identify the field polarities. If they are not, use paint or permanent marker to mark them. Paper correction fluid also works quite well.

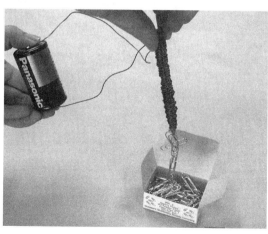

Sometime in every student's education, he or she should experiment with an electromagnet. A large nail wrapped with wire, a battery, and a box of paperclips allows students to explore magnetism and its properties.

Questions for review can include the following:
- How can you form an electric magnet using wire and a battery?
- How does a magnet affect other magnets?

- What kinds of materials are attracted to magnets?
- How does a compass work?
- How are permanent magnets and electric magnets similar? How are they different?
- How does the magnetic field produced by an electric magnet compare to a magnetic field produced by a permanent magnet? Will one type affect the other type?
- In what direction does the magnetic field extend out from a coil of wire?

Suggestions for Presentation

There are a variety of plans for the production of simple motors. The plan for this motor has been successful with students of all ages because of the minimal material requirements and the ease of building it. Students can work alone or in pairs to assemble this piece. The method of explaining the assembly procedure can also vary according to the needs and abilities of the students.

A few methods you might use include the following:
- Copy the assembly instructions in this paper and give them out as handouts for students to follow.
- Make a large poster that shows each step of the assembly process.
- Guide students though the assembly process step-by-step as a demonstration. Perform each step and have students repeat the procedure for themselves. As students proceed, keep an eye on their progress. When everyone has completed one step, go on to the next one.
- Set a completed model on a demonstration table and show students how it works. Set out an assortment of materials and have students build their own version. They can examine the model and make changes to try to increase its efficiency.

Due to the imbalance of the coil and the repulsive nature of magnetism, the coils tend to jump off the support bars rather frequently. After students have completed the initial assembly, you could hold a short contest to see whose motor can stay running for the longest time. Have students do some brainstorming to design ways to keep the coil seated on the support posts.

Interactive questions for discussion after the motors have been successfully assembled include the following:
- When you hold the coil in the energized position on the supports, what type of force is exerted between the coil and the permanent magnet?
- Is the coil attracted or repelled to the permanent magnet?
- Is there a position in which the coil is attracted to the permanent magnet?
- What happens to the magnet field when the enameled part of the wire is touching the support?

- As the coil spins on the supports, describe what happens when the coil gets a push from the magnet?
- What would happen to the motion of the coil if it did not get a push each time it turned on the supports?
- How can we get the coil to spin in the opposite direction? (There are two ways.)

Another part of this demonstration shows a method for improving the efficiency of this motor. This requires a second magnet to increase the magnet field near the coil. Have students hold the second magnet about ½ inch above the spinning coil. When the coil is energized, it will push against both magnets. If the magnet is held close enough, a student can feel the force applied between the magnet and magnetized coil.

If you flip the handheld magnet over, it will attract the coil instead of repelling it. When you bring the magnet near the coil, it will slow down or even stop the coil movement.

Students can also experiment with altering the shape of the motor coil. I call the coil the St. Valentine's Day Special. Other shapes could be ovals, squares, triangles, and figure eights. Students will have to rebalance the coil, but most shapes will still work.

The double-coiled motor

After you have demonstrated and explained the simple motor, have a short discussion about the similarities between the fields exerted by electric magnets and the permanent magnets. If someone questions whether the permanent magnet can be replaced with another coil, it is a good lead-in for students to explore this possibility. Most successful student-designed models will use a separate battery for each coil.

Don't introduce the double-coiled motor shown in this section until students have had the opportunity to try building their own version. In most cases, students will opt for keeping the bottom coil energized all the time. The double-coiled motor is built with the two coils acting in series. You may need to review series circuits before or during this demonstration to students.

Interactive questions and discussion of the double-coiled motor could include the following:

- How are the simple motor and the double-coiled motor similar?
- How are the simple motor and the double-coiled motor different?
- Trace the flow of electricity from beginning to end for the double-coiled motor.
- What might be some advantages or disadvantages of this type of motor?
- Which setup for the motor will require more electricity to operate?

Postdemonstration Activities and Discussion

The directions in this article call for scraping all the enamel off one wire and half the enamel from the wire on the other side. Students will find it amazing to discover that coil will still turn if both sides are scraped clean. They can try this with their original coil or make a second one and scrape both protruding wires completely clean. This setup works because the coil bounces upward during the magnetic "push" and breaks the electric circuit.

Scrape the enamel off of both ends.

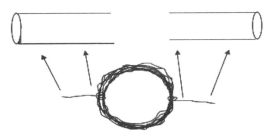

Hans Oersted's (1777–1851) famous discovery showed electricity could form magnetic fields and that the direction of the lines of force radiates perpendicular from the wire. Students can build a tangent galvanometer to show the magnetic field produced by coil and battery.

This coil of wire is wrapped around a compass and then energized by a battery. The compass needle will spin a few turns and then settle down to sit perpendicular to the coil. It demonstrates that the magnetic fields can run through the coil and form directly perpendicular from the wire instead of parallel to it as was earlier thought. The field increases with the number of turns in the coil.

Discussion of Results

The simple motor works because electricity travels through the coil of wire and temporarily forms a magnetic field. This magnetic field forms only when the bare wire touches the metal supports. The field shuts off when the enameled side of the coil wire is touching the supports because the flow of electricity is interrupted. The flow resumes again as the coil turns back into the position where a magnetic field is produced. You can feel the magnetic repulsion by holding the coil in place with the shiny ends down against the metal supports.

When the coil becomes energized, it will push away from the ceramic magnet with enough force to turn through one revolution. The turning coil has enough rotational inertia to keep it turning though the position of no magnetic field. As the coil continues to turn, it returns to the position where it becomes charged again. The coil gets another push as it passes through the magnetic field once more. This process repeats itself over and over as the motor continues to spin. The action can be very rapid and may be occurring up to 10 times per second.

The double-coiled motor operates on the same principle as the simple motor. The obvious difference is that the ceramic magnet has been replaced with an electric magnet made with a coil of wire. What is not obvious is that both coils are hooked up in a series with electricity flowing through one coil and then the other. The motor coil acts as an on-off switch as it does for the simple motor. Now when the bare wires of motor coil makes contact with the supports, electricity flows, and both coils become electric magnets. The magnet fields repel each other, causing the motor to turn. When the motor coil turns far enough and breaks the circuit, both coils shut off. The motor coil has enough rotational inertia to continue turning and both coils become energized again. The process repeats itself over and over to keep the motor spinning.

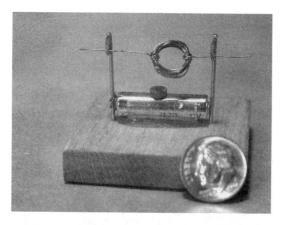

Additional Activities

Here are a few more possible additions to the simple motor design.

How small can these types of motors be made? You can see the small size by looking at the dime in front of this little motor. It was made with a small battery sold for hearing aid use. The coil was made by wrapping the wire around a pencil. It spins just as well as a larger one.

How large can they get? The larger size allows for easier viewing when you are discussing the principles of its operation, so this size works well as a teacher demonstration piece. The coil was made by wrapping 18 feet of copper bell wire around a soda can. The magnet was glued to the base. The supports can be long bolts or nails. Electrical wire fittings were added to the top of the bolts for the coil to reside in.

Directions for Assembly

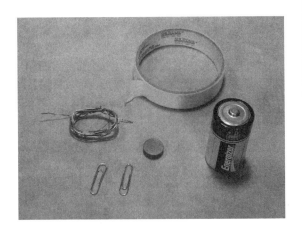

Student Motors

Materials

- 1 D-cell battery
- 1 small magnet
- 1 piece of enameled copper wire, 20 gauge, 50 in. long
- 2 paper clips
- masking or plastic tape

Directions

1. The armature is the first step in the production of this simple motor.

   Start by straightening out any kinks in the enameled copper wire. Next, bend a 2-inch portion of the wire to form a 90-degree turn. Using your thumb to hold the bent portion of the wire against the side of the battery, wrap the rest of the wire around the battery to form a coil.

2. Remove the coil from the battery while holding it together between thumb and forefinger. Wrap the extended wire 2 to 3 times around the coil to hold it together. The coiled-up wire should have a short piece protruding on opposite sides of the coil. Wrap this second wire around the coil also.

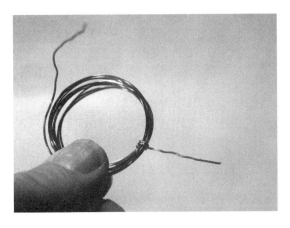

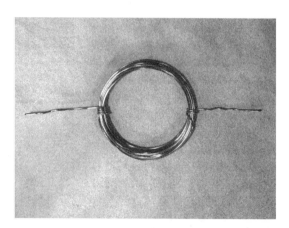

3. With the wire wrapped around both sides of the coil, check to see that they are directly opposite each other. If the ends protrude more than 1 inch from the coil, it can be trimmed or wrapped as extra turns around the coil. Straighten out the 2 protruding wires as much as possible. Extra bumps may hinder the movement.

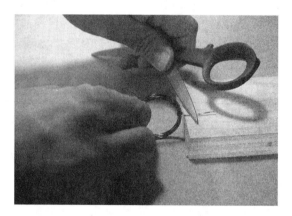

4. Lay one of the ends of the wire flat against a hard surface such as a piece of plywood. Use the sharp edge of the scissors to scrape the enamel off the protruding wires. Turn the coil as you are scraping and remove all the enamel completely off the entire length of this side. Note the wire on the other side of the coil will differ significantly in the directions given in step 5.

5. The preferred method of production is to remove the enamel from just the top half of the second side of the coil. Hold the coil vertically with one hand and lay the other side of the wire against the hard surface. It is important that you scrape only the top half of this piece of wire. The bottom portion of the protruding wire should remain coated with the enamel. (See the drawing on the next page.)

Look at the additional activities section for information on making another coil with both protruding wires stripped clean of enamel. In this instance, the enamel is scraped off of this wire all the way around.

The top half of this wire is scraped clean; the bottom half of the wire still has the enamel left on it.

The enamel is scraped off of this wire all the way around

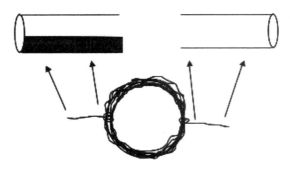

6. The coil is going to be supported on 2 bent paper clips. To make these holders, start by unbending the center portion of both paper clips. Try to straighten out the center of the clip as much as possible.

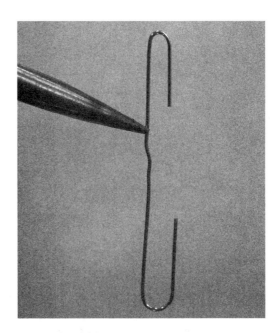

7. Use a set of needle-nosed pliers to firmly grasp the bottom half of the small end of the paper clip.

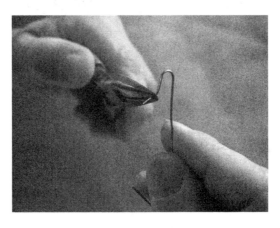

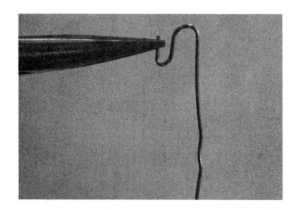

8. Use the pliers to bend a small portion of the paper clip upward to form a small U-shaped channel for the armature to sit in. Repeat this activity for the second paper clip.

The larger bent U sections of the paper clips are bent outward to form more of a V shape.

After the motor is working, the U section can be bent into an O shape. This will help to keep the motor from jumping off the supports.

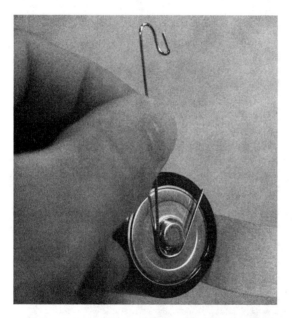

9. Use a few pieces of masking or plastic tape to hold the whole motor together. Tear off a 2-inch portion of tape and use this to attach the first paper clip to the side of the battery. The little knob on the battery should fit into the V portion of the paper clip. Position the second paper clip on the opposite side of the battery using another piece of tape.

10. Both paper clip supports should have the bend at the same height, or the armature will fall off the support as it is spinning. The magnet is placed directly on top of the battery; it should be centered between the 2 paper clips. A piece of tape can be used between the battery and the table surface to keep the battery from rolling over during its operation.

11. Set the coil into the small folds of the paper clips, and make sure that it is balanced. If the coil does not turn evenly, bend the protruding wires to make it balanced. Give the coil a gentle push to get it to start spinning. If it does not spin, try spinning it in the opposite direction. Also, squeeze the paper clip posts tight against the sides of the battery to make sure they are making a good connection.

You can bend the ends of the protruding wire to help keep the coil centered over the magnet.

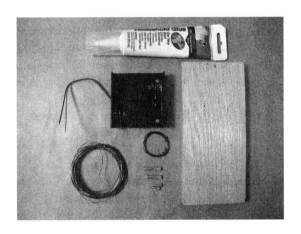

Two-Coil Motors

Materials

- battery holder, 2 D-cell
- wood block, 4 x 8 in.
- coil copper wire, 25 ft. of 20-gauge enameled wire
- coil copper wire, 4 ft. of 22 gauge enameled wire
- wire connectors
- screws, ½ in. long
- glue

SAFETY NOTE

When you are completing the wood base, using the following safety equipment is strongly suggested:

- Goggles for eye protection. NSTA recommends that you use safety goggles that conform to the ANSI Z87.1 standard and that provide both impact and chemical-splash protection for all science laboratory work.
- Dust mask to guard against breathing in airborne sawdust.
- Gloves whenever power tools are used.

Directions

1. Cut the wood block to an approximate size of 4 by 8 inches. Sand all the edges smooth and paint with 1 or 2 coats of varnish.

2. After the varnish dries, the battery holder can be mounted to the wood block base. Inside the battery holder are holes for mounting screws. Drill pilot holes and attach the battery holder to the base by screwing in the screws.

3. The wire extending out of the battery holder should be only about 2 inches long. Cut off excess wire from the battery holder. The wires should have about ½ inch of plastic insulation removed. Use wire strippers or scissors to remove the plastic coating from the end of the wire.

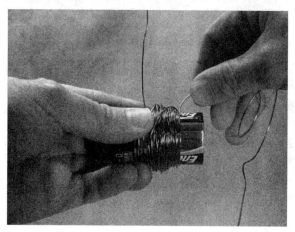

4. The large coil that replaces the permanent magnet is made out of 25 feet of enameled copper wire. Wrap the wire 50 times around a D-cell battery to form the coil. After wrapping the wire around the battery, remove the coil and hold onto it, or the wire will unwind. Press the turns together to pack the wires as tightly as possible.

   Fewer turns might not produce a strong enough magnetic field to spin the coil.

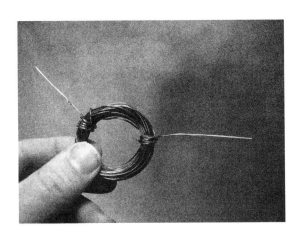

5. Take one of the ends of the wire and wrap it 3 or 4 turns around the coil of wire to hold it together. Tuck the end of the wire under one of the turns and then loop it around to knot it in place.

   The second end of the wire should be wrapped around the opposite side of the coil. It should be placed slightly above the center of the coil instead of directly across from the first side. This space will be used by another wire that is added in step 8.

   Cut both wire ends down to about 3 inches in length.

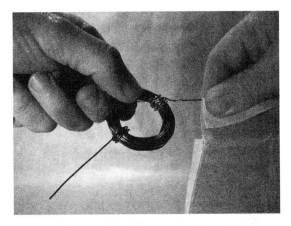

6. Use sandpaper to remove the enamel from the end of the wire that was just wrapped around the coil. Only about 1 inch of wire needs to be sanded clean.

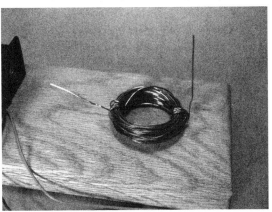

7. Lay the coil down against the wood base. The wire with the end scraped clean will be attached to one of the wires extending out from the battery holder. The other wire from the coil should extend straight up from the base. This wire will form the right side motor coil support.

8. Cut an 8-inch piece of wire from the leftover supply. This wire has been painted white to make it easier to identify it in the pictures. The separate white wire is wrapped around the coil directly opposite from the right side support. Three inches of white wire extend up from the coil. This will form the left side support. The white wire is wrapped around the coil 3 or 4 turns and then tucked under one of the previous turns; this will knot it and hold it in place.

9. The next step is to attach the battery holder using wire connectors. The black wire is shown connected to the scraped wire that extends out from the coil. Stick each end of the wires to be joined into the opposite ends of the connector. You must squeeze the connector hard with pliers; this will lock the wires together. Sand the end of the white wire to remove the white paint and the enamel. Then join this wire to the red wire from the battery holder. Once again, use a connector to join the 2 wires together.

10. Bend the wire supports for the motor into a sideways S shape. To get this shape, bend the top inch of both wires down toward the base. The next step is to bend the last ½ inch of these wires back up again as shown in the picture. Both of the U-shaped slots should be at the same level or the motor will slide toward the lower side.

11. Remove the enamel from the bottom portion of the U-shaped slot. To do so, rub it with some sandpaper or a nail file until the copper wire is scraped clean. If any enamel is left in this area, it will prevent the coil from completing the electric circuit when it needs to.

12. Glue the coil to the wood base. Use a silicone adhesive and apply it liberally to the bottom of the coil. Set the coil down onto the wood base in the intended position, and then press lightly to spread the glue onto the wood surface.

13. This coil is made the same way as the one used in the simple motor. The only difference is that this coil is smaller. Wrap the wire around a C cell–sized battery. About 15 to 18 turns is satisfactory. Refer back to the simple motor plans for complete instructions on how to make the coil.

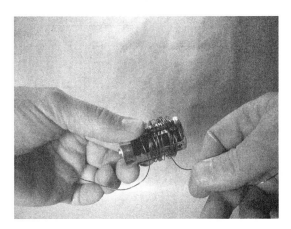

14. The coil for this motor needs to be finely balanced for it to operate. The magnetic field generated by the bottom coil is not as strong as the one produced by a permanent magnet.

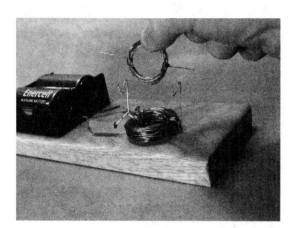

15. With the coil scraped and finely balanced, it is ready to run. Put the batteries in place, lay the coil down into the slots, and give it a spin.

   If the motor coil does not spin or if it spins very slowly, it may be too far away from the bottom coil. Bend the 2 wire supports to bring the coil down closer to the bottom coil. The motor will spin faster when the bottom of the motor coil is level with the top of the edge of the lower coil.

Instructional Information

Overview

Filament Board

Part one. A 150-watt lightbulb has had the glass globe removed from it, exposing the tungsten filament in the metal base. This filament is wired in series with a second small lightbulb and a 9-volt battery. When the circuit is complete, the small light will glow brightly. A lit match is then held to the exposed tungsten filament. As the filament gets red hot, the small bulb can be observed getting very dim and then going out. When the match is taken away and the filament cools, the small bulb can be observed getting brighter again.

Part two. The 150-watt bulb is replaced with a tungsten filament from a 60-watt bulb. When the small bulb is screwed in its base, it remains lit for a few moments and then goes out. When a person blows gently across the exposed filament of the large bulb, the small light will once again light up and continues to do so as long as air is directed across the device. As the filament heats, the resistance in the tungsten increases enough to keep the small bulb from lighting.

Jelly Jar Lightbulb

The principle of a lightbulb can be demonstrated without the danger of creating a vacuum inside a glass jar. One of the difficulties in demonstrating a lightbulb centers on the removal of air from the chamber using a vacuum pump. This device suggests two alternative methods. The first method uses several lit candles inside a jar to burn up as much of the available oxygen as possible before turning on the power. The second method is to release helium into the jar. This lighter-than-air gas will push most of the air out of the bottom of the container. The mechanical pencil "lead" filaments may last up to 2 minutes before burning out with these methods.

Student Skills

Observation.
- Students can observe that heating the tungsten wire will cause the small lightbulb to go out.
- Students can observe the cooling effect of blowing on the bare filament of the large bulb, allowing the small bulb to get brighter.
- Students can observe the basic operation of a lightbulb.

Draw a Conclusion. As students watch the use of the filament board, they can conclude that heating or cooling a metal can change the flow of electricity through it. As students watch the operation of a lightbulb, they can define some of the requirements for a successful operation. Students should be able to identify some of the problems that were obstacles in constructing the lightbulb designed by Thomas Edison.

Trial and Error. Students can attempt some additional experiments with electricity, such as building simple circuits.

Related Concepts or Processes

Electricity	Resistance
Series and parallel circuits	Thermal energy
Properties of matter	Light
Voltage	AC/DC

Prior Knowledge

Students should have some basic understanding of electricity and some related concepts. The flow of electricity requires a complete path and that more than one object can be connected in the circuit. The pathway or circuit for electricity to follow can be wired either in series or in parallel. How these differ in the flow of electricity will also depend on the number of objects wired into a circuit.

Although it may not be necessary to have a working knowledge of Ohm's law, it would be helpful if students know that resistance can impede the flow of electricity.

Predemonstration Discussion

The filament board and the lightbulb are both helpful as a supplemental demonstration when you are teaching about the flow of electricity, series circuits, and resistance. They are most effective after students have built simple circuits using batteries, bulbs, and wire.

Questions for review could include the following:
- What is a complete circuit?
- What happens to the flow of electrons if the circuit is broken?
- How does a lightbulb work?
- Why are we unable to light a large lightbulb with a small battery?
- What do you think would happen if we tried to light a small lightbulb with a higher voltage than needed?

If you will be testing helium inside the lightbulb, a few questions to ask might include the following:
- Why does a helium balloon float?
- What gas is needed for a candle to burn?
- What happens to a candle if it is placed in an overturned jar?
- Why does it take a while for it to go out?
- What would happen if a candle is placed into a jar of helium?

Short demonstrations can be set up to answer the last two questions. Try placing a jar over a lit birthday candle until the candle goes out. Use a balloon to fill an overturned jar with helium by gently releasing helium from the mouth of the balloon into the mouth of the jar. This jar can then be placed over a lit candle causing the candle to go out much more quickly than when the jar is filled with air.

Suggestions for Presentation

Filament Board

Before using this piece, it is very helpful to check the condition of the 9-volt battery you are using. Nothing can ruin this experiment more thoroughly than the bulb failing to light when it is supposed to. Unscrewing the small bulb to act as an on-off switch is easiest. Before screwing this bulb back in, ask students to examine the circuit and determine if it is in series or parallel.

This part of the experiment uses the device and the 150-watt filament. Screw the small bulb into the holder and observe that it stays lit. Holding a lit match to the exposed filament will make it glow a bright red. As this occurs, the small bulb will get dimmer and dimmer. Remove the match and note that the bulb gets brighter. Repeat the action while discussing possible reasons for the observations.

After a short discussion, it is time to perform the second part of this demonstration.

Replace the 150-watt exposed filament with the 60-watt filament. Screw the small bulb into its socket and quickly move your hand away. Students should notice that the bulb remains lit for a few seconds before going out. Repeat this step if everyone was not able to make this observation.

Ask a student to take a deep breath and then blow across the exposed filament. The bulb should light as long as there is some air movement. The moment the student stops blowing, the small bulb will go out again.

After discussing the relationship between temperature and resistance, have someone very carefully touch the exposed filament and explain his or her observation to the class.

Interactive questions for discussion could include the following:
* Is the path of the electricity on the filament board a series or parallel circuit?
* What is meant by a series circuit?
* What does the term *resistance* mean?
* Resistance can be thought of as an internal friction impeding the flow of electrons. What is the result of friction?
* What usually causes bulbs to get dimmer when powered by a battery?
* What do you think the heat is doing to the flow of electricity?

- As the tungsten wire cools, what happens to the flow of electricity?
- How do we know if electricity is flowing in this circuit?
- What is a common method for cooling objects or liquids that are too hot?
- Why does blowing across the filament make small bulbs light up?
- What is the air doing to the hot filament?
- What does blowing on the exposed filament do to the resistance of the tungsten wire?
- If we see the bulb lit for a few moments and then see it go out, what might be the explanation for this action?
- How did the two filaments differ in their respective demonstrations.
- Which filament allows more electricity to flow?

Jelly Jar Lightbulb

The lightbulb can be used before or after using the filament. One piece can enhance the other. Before setting up the lightbulb, show students several different shapes, sizes, and power ratings for a variety of lightbulbs.

The exposed filament from the 150-watt bulb can be reviewed and compared to the basic setup found in the jelly jar lightbulb.

Ask students to trace the pathway the electricity follows as it flows through a lightbulb.

SAFETY NOTE

Glass will be warm and the filament, alligator clips, and wire inside the jar get hot. Allow all parts to cool adequately before dismantling and handling.

Interactive questions for discussion during the presentations could include the following:
- Does it matter which direction the electrons flow through a lightbulb?
- What does *DC* or *direct current* mean?
- What does *AC* or *alternating current* mean?
- What are the similarities found between the jelly jar lightbulb and one that is commercially produced?
- What is the purpose of the glass bulb?
- Why does the oxygen have to be removed from inside the lightbulb?
- What is the purpose of repeatedly burning the candles before the jar is assembled?

Postdemonstration Activities and Discussion

- Explain why the filament board experiment must be set up in series. What would be the result if it were tried as a parallel circuit?

- Have students research Thomas Edison's invention of the lightbulb.
- Why was the invention of the lightbulb such an important historical milestone?
- How has the lightbulb changed in the last 100 years?

> **SAFETY NOTE**
> Take great care with the hot flame and hot wax when working near a lit candle flame.

The amount of resistance that a wire has to the flow of electricity can be measured using an ohmmeter. The units are *ohms*. To measure the resistance across the filament, touch the meter's wire leads to the bottom of the lightbulb base. The increase in resistance can be observed and measured when the tungsten filament is held in the flame of a candle. The filament will glow red from the heat of the match. The filament will not be damaged due to tungsten's high melting point. If dry ice is available, it can be used to cool the tungsten filament. If the wire is sufficiently cooled, it will show a decrease in resistance across the filament according to the ohmmeter.

Discussion of Results

Filament Board

The small lightbulb is rated at 1.5 volts, and yet we are using a 9-volt battery to light it. If this bulb were wired directly to the battery without the additional filament, it would burn out within a few moments. This is telling us that the filament has a large amount of resistance to the flow of electricity and allows only a portion of it to flow.

The resistance inside the tungsten wire can turn some of the energy into heat. It is not nearly hot enough to make this exposed filament glow, but it can be felt as a hot wire. The temperature increases on the filament because of the flow of electricity through it. As the temperature goes up, the resistance increases. When the resistance becomes high enough, insufficient energy reaches the small bulb to light it. The cooling effect of blowing on the wire drops the temperature of the filament; the resistance is lowered temporarily, and enough energy can move through the wire to light the little bulb.

Jelly Jar Lightbulb

The operation of the lightbulb enhances the concept of resistance shown with the filament board. The filament of a modern lightbulb uses a small coiled wire made of tungsten because its melting point is 3422°C or 6192°F, the highest of any metallic element. As electricity passes through the wire, the tungsten tries to hold on to the electrons passing though it. The electrons have to be forced through due to this resistance. Tungsten has 400 times more resistance than copper wire. Some of this force is absorbed by the metal and is changed into heat. As more electricity passes through the filament, the metal filament gets hotter and hotter until the metal glows white-hot. The metal gives off light because the heat energy causes the electrons in the atoms to become very energetic and move away from the nucleus of the tungsten atoms. Electrons eventually lose some of their energy and move back closer to the nucleus. As the electrons lose energy, they release photons, or little bits of light.

A lightbulb must have most of the air (oxygen) removed from it. If it didn't, the wire filament would burn up in a few seconds. When a lightbulb eventually "burns out," it is because the filament slowly vaporizes until the circuit is broken and electricity no longer flows. The vaporized tungsten actually re-solidifies on the sides of the glass bulb during the bulb's working lifetime.

The jelly jar lightbulb uses a carbon rod as a filament because of its high melting point, (3550°C or 6422°F) and because it is easily obtainable. This lightbulb filament lasts for only a few minutes because the burning candles cannot use up all of the available oxygen inside the jar. Although there is not enough available oxygen to support combustion of the candles, there is enough to slowly burn up the filament. This is one of the problems that Thomas Edison had while trying to design his own lightbulb. Many of the filaments would either melt due to a low melting point or they would burn up in the oxygen inside the globe.

Additional Activities

Students may be interested in seeing the inside of a three-way lightbulb. Dissect a 50-100-150 watt lightbulb in the same manner as preparing a bulb for the filament board. A three-way bulb has 2 filaments in it. When a lamp is on the lowest setting, one filament comes on (it is usually listed as a 50-watt filament). On the second setting (usually a 100-watt filament) the other filament will light up. On the highest setting both filaments come on, for a total of 150 watts.

Directions for Assembly

Filament Board

Materials

- 1 wood for base, 6 in. × 12 in.
- 1 large lightbulb base
- 1 lightbulb, 60 watts
- 1 lightbulb, 150 watts
- 1 miniature lightbulb base
- 1 miniature lightbulb, 1.5 V
- 2 screws, # 6–8, ¾ in.
- 4 screws, # 4, ½ in.
- 9-V battery holder with wiring harness
- 9-V battery
- bell wire, approximately 13 in. tape, masking, plastic, or duct
- glue

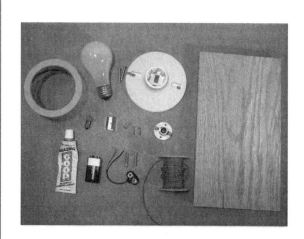

Directions

1. This project begins with the wooden block. Cut the wood into a piece about 6 inches by 12 inches. Then sand all surfaces and paint the wood with varnish. You might want to sign and date the bottom of the block.

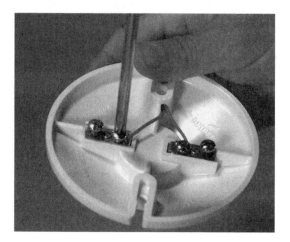

2. The large lightbulb base has the wire connecting screws mounted on the bottom side. Turn the piece over and loosen the connecting screws. Two wires are needed: One should be 5 inches long and the other about 8 inches long. Strip ½ inch of insulation off both ends on each wire. Wrap one of the bare ends of a wire around a connecting screw and then tighten the screw down against the wire to hold it tight. Repeat for the second wire.

3. Thread the 2 wires under or through a hole in the bulb base. Use two ¾-inch screws to mount the 110-volt lightbulb base onto the right side of the wood block.

4. Bend the bare end of the 8-inch wire from the large bulb base around the connecting nut on the small lightbulb base. Tighten the screw to hold the wire in place. Use two ½-inch screws to mount the miniature lightbulb base onto the left side of the wood base.

   Use two ½-inch screws to mount the 9-volt battery holder onto the wood base. It should be located between the lightbulb bases, but not in a direct line.

5. Wire the battery harness and lightbulb bases in series. Attach 1 wire from the battery harness to the second connecting screw on the small bulb base. Attach this wire by wrapping the bare end around the screw and then tighten it to hold it fast.

   The other wire from the harness is connected to the 5-inch wire extending from the large bulb base. To connect these 2 wires, insert the bare ends into a wire tube connecter. Use pliers to tightly squeeze the tube connecter, this should permanently join the wires.

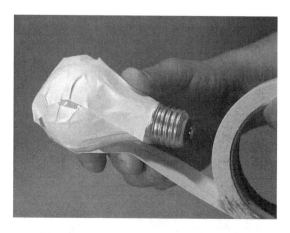

6. Remove the filament from a 60-watt bulb and the 150-watt bulb very carefully because the tungsten wire is very fragile and easily broken. Start with one of the bulbs. Remove the glass from the lightbulb base. The following steps will keep the glass from shattering. Use masking tape and completely cover the bulb with a layer of the tape. This will allow the bulb to break but keep the pieces intact until it can be disposed of.

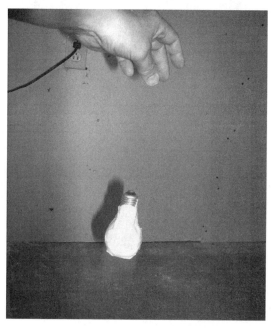

7. Drop the bulb onto a hard surface from a height of about 2 to 3 feet; this should be enough to break the bulb.

SAFETY NOTE

In this series of instructions, wear safety goggles for eye protection. Stray bits of glass may come off of the lightbulb, as it is being broken or cleaned with the pliers. NSTA recommends that you use safety goggles that conform to the ANSI Z87.1 standard and that provide both impact and chemical-splash protection for all science laboratory work.

Use gloves when handling glass (the photographs have omitted gloves to make the procedures clearer).

8. Although dropping the bulb should be enough to break the glass, the bulb may not be ready to have the base removed from the glass. Hit the tape-wrapped bulb with pliers to break it into smaller pieces.

9. Carefully remove the broken glass from the metal part of the bulb. If the filament is separated from the wire that supports it, it is possible to carefully unbend the wire support and reattach it.

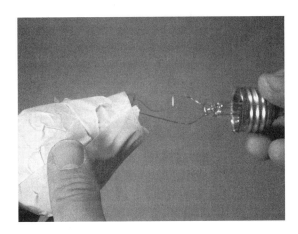

10. Use the pliers to grab and remove any small sharp pieces of glass from the metal bottom of the bulb. Remove all sharp glass edges that extend above the metal.

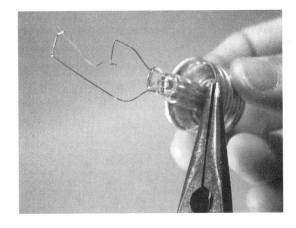

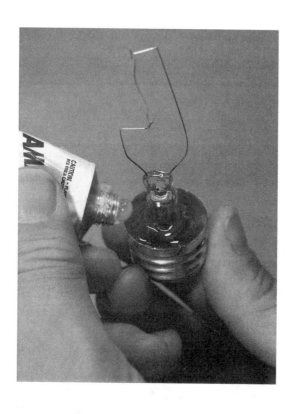

11. Use a hot glue gun or other glue to fill in the empty space in the metal base of the bulb. The glue is needed to give the glass stem additional support inside the metal bulb base. Allow the glue to dry thoroughly before proceeding.

12. The tungsten filament and wires are very fragile. The support wire will occasionally get bent through use. You can put the filament and wires back into position by bending them carefully up again. The filament can also become detached. You can unbend the very tips of the support wires and then bend them around the tungsten filament again to reattach the filament.

13. Repeat steps 6 through 12 for the second lightbulb.

14. It is now time to complete the assembly and test the device. Start by screwing the 60-watt lightbulb filament into the large lightbulb base. Next, attach the 9-volt battery head to the battery holder and harness.

15. Screw the 1.5-volt bulb into the small bulb base. It should shine for about 5 seconds and then go out. To test the circuit, blow directly on the large bulb filament. The small bulb should shine very brightly as long as you are blowing on the filament. During operation, the exposed filament is hot to the touch. It can be touched, but do so very gently or the wire may break.

16. You can also test the 150-watt filament in the large lightbulb base. When it is screwed in, the 1.5-volt bulb will remain lit.

17. Unscrew the 1.5-volt bulb immediately after any demonstrations. If you forget to remove it, the next time you try this experiment the 9-volt battery will most likely be dead and will need to be replaced.

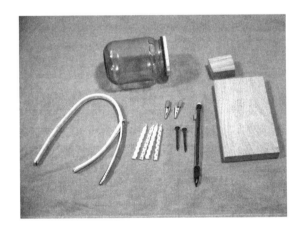

Jelly Jar Lightbulb
Materials

- alligator clips
- 2 wood screws, 1 in. long
- 1 wood block, 4 in. × 6 in.
- 1 wood block, 1½ in. square
- 1 piece copper wire, 12/2 or 14/2, 1 ft. long
- 3 birthday candles
- mechanical pencil lead
- small jar with lid

SAFETY NOTE
The jar should be large enough to have at least 1½ inches of clearance from the filament to all sides and 2 inches clearance to the top of the jar. Placing the filament too close to a glass surface will cause it to get hot.

For a quick demonstration setup, the bulb can be constructed without the wooden square and without the wooden base. An easy alternative is to use modeling clay to hold the candles in place inside the jar instead of the wooden disc. Add more clay on the outside of the lid to seal the holes that the wires come through and to make the jar sit up straight.

Directions

1. Use a chisel to cut 2 grooves in a piece of wood that will be used as the base. The grooves are for the wires that are coming out of the lid of the jar. The grooves will allow the wires to lie under the lid and then allow the lid to fit flat against the wood base.

2. The small wood block can either be square or rounded, depending on your preference. It should be small enough to fit inside the jar mouth without coming in contact with the glass material of the container. Drill 2 holes through the small square block for the wires to come through. They should be placed toward the center of the block and should be spaced about ¾ inch apart from each other. The drill bit size should be approximately the same size as the wire diameter to give the wire a snug fit when it is positioned inside the block.

3. Drill 2 holes through the jar lid. These holes should be about ¼ inch in diameter. They should be located toward the middle of the lid and spaced ¾ of an inch apart. The holes should match up with the 2 holes in the small wooden block. The holes should position the block in the middle of the lid. Check to see that the block will not interfere with the jar's being screwed onto the lid.

Remove the lid from the jar before drilling.

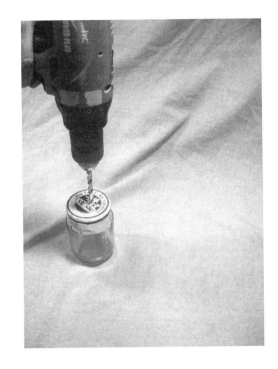

SAFETY NOTE

For this series of instructions, the following safety equipment is strongly recommended:

• Goggles for eye protection. NSTA recommends that you use safety goggles that conform to the ANSI Z87.1 standard and that provide both impact and chemical-splash protection for all science laboratory work.

• Dust mask to guard against breathing in airborne sawdust.

• Gloves whenever power tools are used.

4. Use a utility knife to cut the sheathing of a 1-foot piece of housing wire. Either 12/2 gauge or 14/2 gauge will work fine. Cover the wires needed inside with another coating of plastic insulation. Use wire strippers to remove a ½-inch piece of insulation from both ends of each wire.

5. After the ends of the wire are stripped, thread both pieces through the holes drilled into the lids, and then through the holes in the block.

6. Extend the wire up through the block about 2 inches. Then make 2 90-degree bends in the wires underneath the lid. The lid should fit flush against the wood base with the wires extending out from underneath it in the chiseled channel.

7. Drill 2 screw holes into the wood disc and lid. Drill 1 hole to the side of the wires instead of going between them. This will keep the drill bit from accidentally removing the plastic insulation on the wires. A counter sink drill bit should be used. This will allow the screw heads to be flush with the block surface. Then screw down the block and lid against the wood base, holding them firmly in place.

8. Drill 4 holes for holding the birthday candles. The diameter of the hole should be slightly smaller than the diameter of the candles to be used. Drill the holes in each corner of the block, about ½-inch deep.

9. Don't have all 4 birthday candles at the same height. Use scissors to cut one of the candles in half. Squeeze the 2 longer birthday candles and the 2 half-candles into each of the holes drilled to hold them on the block.

10. The 2 alligator clips should fit snuggly onto the wire protruding up through the block. They should be positioned about 1 to 2 inches from the top of the jar when it is screwed down against the lid.

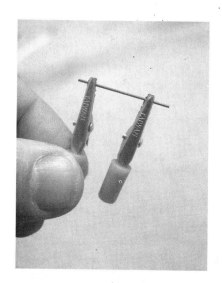

11. The filament is 1 inch of common mechanical pencil "lead." This filament is really a small carbon rod and is extremely fragile. It is easier to attach to the 2 alligator clips and the carbon rod together when they are not on the base. The alligator clips should be about ¾ inch apart, holding the carbon in the first set of teeth on the clips.

12. Gently slide the 2 alligator clips and carbon rod assembly back onto the 2 wires extending up from the wood block.

13. With the lightbulb base ready to go, it is now time to try and remove some of the excess oxygen from the inside the jar. Light a large candle and bring the inside of the jar down over the flame. Move the jar around to place the candle in various positions inside the jar before the candle flame goes out. Place the jar mouth down against the table and relight the large candle and repeat this extinguishing process again. Light the small candles on the base and relight the large candle one more time. Repeat the step once more with the large candle. The more oxygen that is burned up by the candles, the longer the lightbulb will work.

14. After the large candle is extinguished for the third time, quickly move the jar over to the lightbulb base and place it over the small candles. The small candles should extinguish rather quickly since there is little oxygen left in the jar. Screw the jar down against the metal lid.

You can use helium to replace the air in the lightbulb jar instead of using the burning candles. Helium balloons or small helium supply canisters are available at most craft stores. To fill the jar with helium, carefully untie the knot in the balloon and hold the mouth closed to prevent the release of the gas. Hold the jar with the mouth facing down while slowly releasing some of the gas into the jar (about half of the balloon). Helium is less dense than air, so it will float up in the jar and displace most of the air residing there.

Quickly screw the jar down on the base. The lightbulb is now ready to test.

15. The bulb needs 6 to 12 volts to light it up. A battery charger is a good way to supply the correct voltage to the bulb. The alligator clips from the charger are attached to the wires that run inside the bulb. A 6- or 12-volt lantern battery is another possible source of power.

16. Turn out the lights and turn on the power to the bulb. The carbon rod will smoke a little bit and then will glow with a brilliant white light.

The power source will determine the brightness of the bulb and the length of time that it will remain lit. A battery charger will produce a very bright light but may last for only 1 to 2 minutes. A lantern battery will not produce as bright a light, but the filament will last significantly longer.

SAFETY NOTE

The glass will be warm and the filament and wires inside will be very hot. Make sure all parts have cooled adequately before anyone handles them.

RESOURCES

Berry, D.A. 1987. *A potpourri of physics teaching ideas.* College Park, MD: American Association of Physics Teachers.

Doughty, P. 1991. *Science snackbook.* San Francisco: The Exploratorium.

Edge, R. 1981. *String and sticky tape experiments.* College Park, MD: American Association of Physics Teachers.

Faughn, T. A. 1991. *Physical science.* Philadelphia: Saunders College.

Freier, G. D. and F.J. Anderson. 1981. *A demonstration handbook for physics.* College Park, MD: American Association of Physics Teachers.

Graf, R. 1964. *Safe and simple electrical experiments.* Mineola, NY: Dover.

Hewitt, P. 1998. *Conceptual physics for parents and teachers.* Newburyport, MA: Focus Publishing.

Liem, T. 1981. *Invitations to scientific inquiry.* El Cajon, CA: Science Inquiry Enterprises.

Macaulay, D. 1988. *The way things work.* Boston: Houghton Mifflin.

McDermott, L. 1996. *Physics by inquiry, Vol. I.* Hoboken, NJ: John Wiley.

McDermott, L. 1996. *Physics by inquiry, Vol. II.* Hoboken, NJ: John Wiley.

Morrow, W. 1985. *Raceways: Having fun with balls and tracks.* New York: Addison Wesley.

Renner, A.G. 1974. *How to make and use electric motors.* New York: Putnam.

Ronan, C. A. 1996. *Science explained.* New York: Henry Holt.

Taylor, B. A. P., J. Poth, and D. J. Portman. 1995. *Teaching physics with toys.* New York: Tab Books.

Materials Resources

American Scientific Products
1430 Waukegan Rd.
McGraw Park, IL 60085
(312) 689-8410

Arbor Scientific
P. O. Box 2750
Ann Arbor, MI 48106-2750
(313) 663-3733 .

Edmund Scientific
101 East Gloucester Pike
Barrington, NJ 08007
(609) 573-6257

Educational Innovations
362 Main Ave.
Norwalk, CT 06851
(888) 912-7474

Fisher Scientific
4901 W. LeMoyne St.
Chicago, IL 60651
(312) 378-7770

Frey Scientific
905 Hickory Lane
P. O. Box 8101
Mansfield, OH 44901-8101
(419) 589-9905

Kelvin
280 Adams Blvd.
Farmington, NY 11735
(800) 535-8469

Nasco
901 Janesville Ave.
Fort Atkinson, WI 53538
(414) 563-2446

PASCO Scientific
10101 Foothills Blvd.
P. O. Box 619011
Roseville, CA 95661-9011
(916) 786-3800

Rudolph Instruments
40 Pier Lane
Fairfield, NJ 07004
(201) 227-0139

Sargent-Welch Scientific
7300 North Linder Ave.
P. O. Box 1026
Skokie, IL 60077
(312) 677-0600

Schoolmasters Science
745 State Circle
P. O. Box 1941
Ann Arbor, MI 48106
(313) 761-5072

Science Kit and Boreal Laboratories
777 East Park Dr.
Tonawanda, NY 14151-5003
(800) 828-7777

Steve Spangler Science
3930 South Kalamath St.
Englewood, CO 80110
(303) 798-2778

Research Review

"Education is not rocket science. It's harder," according to an old adage. This may be true, especially if education is successful. Today, with the pressure applied to teachers by state and federal mandated programs and testing, the stakes could not be any greater for helping students meet the standards set forth through these programs. Projects such as the National Science Education Standards (NSES) (NRC 1996) and Project 2061 developed by the American Association for Advancement of Science (1993) have described a basic core of understanding and abilities that all students should process, but helping students attain that core is not easy. To do so, teachers must use a variety of teaching methods and practices.

Among the areas of concern revealed by research on educational practice are
- The importance of prior knowledge,
- Active learning methods of instruction,
- Doing demonstrations in the classroom, and
- Touching exhibits to supplement instruction.

The Importance of Prior Knowledge

Research shows us that students learn more effectively when they already know something about content and when concepts mean something to them and to their particular background or culture. Prior knowledge can act as a lens through which students view and absorb new information. It is a composite of what people are, based on what they have learned from their academic and everyday experiences (Kujawa and Huske 1995).

According to Good and Brophy (1997), construction of new knowledge goes more smoothly when learners can relate new theories and content to their existing background knowledge. Bransford, Brown, and Cocking (1999) looked very closely at transfer of understanding and conditions promoting transfer. They found that what students learn is strongly affected by what they already know. Students interpret new experiences in terms of previous knowledge, and missing previous knowledge may be interfering with learning.

When teachers link new information to the student's prior knowledge, they use what students already know as a scaffold that anchors what students are learning. Teachers must activate students' interest and curiosity and infuse instruction with a sense of purpose, giving what the students are learning a more permanent position in their knowledge bases (Willis 1995).

By tapping their students' prior knowledge in all subject areas, teachers can plan lessons that will clarify incomplete or erroneous prior knowledge, determine the extent of instruction necessary in a particular topic area, and discern necessary adjustments to planned independent activities and assessment materials (Kujawa and Huske 1995). Teachers can use class discussions during demonstrations to activate and illustrate students' prior knowledge. Such dialoging and visualizations also encourage students to think about their own thinking—what happens in a particular situation and why—thus transferring the thought process to a conscious level.

Active Learning Methods of Instruction

Good teaching of science creates environments in which teachers and their students work together as active learners. The terms *active learning, experiential learning, hands-on learning, active questioning,* and *Socratic dialogue* represent methods that have been suggested for engaging students' minds in the learning process. They imply that science should be something that students do and in which they should be involved, rather than something that is done to students. In an active learning setting, students describe objects and events, ask questions, answer questions, acquire knowledge, construct explanations of natural phenomena, test their explorations in many different ways, and communicate their ideas.

The National Science Education Standards (NRC 1996), which stand as an educational milestone, define and suggest what constitutes active learning:

The term *active process* implies physical and mental activity. Hands-on activities are not enough; students also must have "minds-on" experiences. Science teaching must involve students in inquiry-oriented investigations in which they interact with their teacher and peers. Students establish connections between their current knowledge of science and the scientific knowledge found in many sources; they apply science content to new questions. They engage in problem solving, planning, decision-making, and group discussions. They experience assessments that are consistent with an active approach to learning. Emphasizing active science learning means shifting away from the teacher presenting information and covering science topics in a passive mode. The perceived need to include all the topics, vocabulary, and information given in textbooks is in direct conflict with the central goal of having students learn scientific knowledge and understanding (pp. 20–21).

Although the NSES emphasize inquiry, they do not recommend a single approach to science teaching. Teachers should use several different strategies to develop the knowledge, understanding, and abilities described in the NSES Content Standards. Performance of hands-on science activities does not guarantee inquiry, nor does reading about science proscribe inquiry.

Research shows that hands-on activities stimulate learning by changing the audience from passive into active participants, but many activities may not be appropriate for students to perform singly or in small groups because of constraints such as setup time, cost, and space. In these cases, teachers can provide active learning with large group instruction, such as lecture demonstrations (Backren 2003).

There are many teaching styles an instructor can use that drive students from passive to active roles. Students can be actively engaged by answering questions, drawing diagrams, writing short explanations of how concepts can be applied, explaining to others what they believe are the key components, and offering situations that demonstrate the given concept. In large student population studies Hake (2003). found that these types of interactive engagement could increase the effectiveness of conceptually difficult courses well beyond the results obtained from more traditional passive lecture methods. McDermott and Redish (1999), although their studies were not as extensive as Hake's, reached the same conclusion. McDermott also found preliminary evidence suggesting that students retain learning for a longer period of time when teachers use interactive engagement. Ideally, an active environment gives students room to interact with materials when possible, to ask questions, and to construct ideas in their own terms (Hayes and Deyhle 2001).

Demonstrations in the Classroom

Using demonstrations to help explain science concepts is not new. In fact, Samuel Johnson said:

> People have now-a-days got a strange opinion that everything should be taught by lectures. Now, I cannot see that lectures can do so much good as reading the books from which the lectures are taken. I know nothing that can best be taught by lectures, except where experiments are to be shown (Boswell 1766).

Until recently, the effectiveness of demonstrations has not been questioned. Research over the last 15 years has shown some good news and some bad news about demonstrations. Compelling evidence suggests demonstrations should continue to share a major role in science education when they are used correctly (Backren 2003). Studies such as that done by Wolff et al. (1997) found several factors that interfered with the effectiveness of demonstrations. Some of the deterrents for students included the following:
- Lack of theoretical background to separate intended observations from noise,
- Interference from other demonstrations,
- Inability to piece together a coherent framework for understanding, and
- Lack of opportunities for testing explanations.

Demonstrations clarify through example and provide a concrete foundation upon which abstractions can be built. The most basic justification for demonstrations is that they can connect concepts with objects and events in the real world. The more closely demonstration pieces resemble objects that students encounter in everyday life, the easier it is for students to access prior knowledge and to construct an understanding of the intended concept (Parkins 1990).

The most recent research suggests that inquiry is the latest and greatest educational trend in science education. It may not be immediately obvious how demonstrations are tied into scientific inquiry. Scientific inquiry as presented in the NSES suggests students' performing experiments and collecting data. That seems diametrically opposed to students' watching a teacher perform a demonstration. However, it is possible and even desirable to keep demonstrations as part of a teacher's repertoire and still address the state and national standards (Gross 2003). The NSES recognize that inquiry is not always the appropriate method of instruction but rather is one of several methods that a teacher should employ. Each of the following instructional practices taken from the book "Inquiry and the National Science Education Standards" (NRC 2003, pp. 165–167, 170–171) adhere to the "…fundamental understandings of Inquiry…" and may use demonstrations as a valid educational experience.

- Identify questions and concepts that guide scientific investigations.
- Demonstrations can be used to prompt student questions about the physical principles of the device that's being used. In many cases, words are not adequate to present a clear picture of the concepts in question. Instead, students need to see the principle in action. Visual observations will help anchor the students' understanding in their own sensory experience.
- Design and conduct scientific investigations.
- Demonstrations can be used to show how various pieces of equipment function and operate. This may show students how to use the equipment for their own investigations, but it may also model how a scientist conducts an experiment. Students can see how the teacher progresses through the steps such as set-up, calibration of equipment, and collection of data.
- Use technology and mathematics as defined by NSES to improve investigations and communications.
- Students should be expected to collect and use data from teacher-led demonstrations. Students can also view two versions of the same demonstration. One version might use low-tech equipment and the second version using more sophisticated methods. Students can then compare the results.
- Formulate and revise scientific explanations and models using logic and evidence. Recognize and analyze alternative explanations and models. Communicate and defend a scientific argument.
- Students can use data collected from demonstrations to review and revise the illustrated concepts. Students may also use collected data as an introduction to concepts not yet introduced.

Tulving (1983) asserted the importance of experienced events in students' ability to judge truthfulness and accuracy. The visual aspect of demonstrations provides a complementary way of understanding a concept.

And finally, Gross found that demonstrations can help convince students that concepts can be counterintuitive, an especially useful function for topics that give rise to misconceptions, such as gravity, inertia, air pressure, and motion. Demonstrations give students the opportunity to compare their preconceptions of physical events with the viewed action.

Touching Exhibits to Supplement Instruction

Demonstrations do not always have to be set up and presented to a class. Alternative suggestions include students' exploring on their own. And a classroom that offers science-related materials for students to examine firsthand could motivate them to go beyond the materials presented within the science curriculum. Children have a natural curiosity and will try these devices when they have the opportunity. Research over the last four decades has discovered the importance of the learning environment to student achievement in learning science (Fraser 1998).

Piaget (1971) suggested that children's desire to interact with their environment begins at a very early age with simple actions such as poking, squeezing, shaking, and moving things. Their intense desire to explore is activated whenever children encounter anything that appeals to their interests. Piaget referred to this as *simple abstractions*. Dropping a piece of wood in water can be an example of a simple abstraction. Once children reach the age of eight, they begin to seek explanations, some of which are not necessarily evident in the object itself. Piaget referred to explaining a physical phenomenon that goes beyond direct observable characteristics as *reflective abstractions*. Predicting whether other objects will sink or float based on the observations of wood in water can be an example of what children might consider at this higher level of learning.

In a study on student attitudes toward subject matter, Tifeten (2003) found student interest markedly increased in an atmosphere that was rich in concrete examples of the subject being taught. The most interesting aspect of Tifeten's research revealed that there is a steady increase of opportunities for science exploration as students progress from elementary to middle school. Opportunities for exploration, along with student interest, sharply decreased as students progressed into high school physics and chemistry classes. One possible suggestion for the deterioration was called the *cost curve*. This curve suggests that, as the price of equipment goes up, the availability of the equipment for student use goes down. By the time students are seniors, their science rooms offer only a minimal amount of materials set out to encourage exploration because of the expensive and fragile nature of equipment often used at higher levels.

Appendix B

Tifeten recommends that you make other material available to encourage students to investigate if expensive equipment must remain locked in cabinets when not in use.

References

American Association for Advancement of Science (AAAS). 1993. *Project 2061: Benchmarks for science literacy*. New York: Oxford University Press.

Backren. J. 2003. Demonstrations can raise conceptual understanding in high school science. Paper presented to AAPT. Retrieved online July 2003, site no longer available, 2003.

Boswell, J. 1766. *The life of Samuel Johnson*. England: Barnes and Noble.

Bransford, J. D., A. L. Brown, and R. R. Cocking, eds. 1999. *How people learn: Brain, mind, experience and school*. Washington, DC: National Academy Press.

Fraser, B. J. 1998. Science learning environments: Assessment, effects and determinants. In *The international handbook of science education*, pp. 527–564.

Garvey, C. 1977. *Play*. Cambridge, MA: Harvard University Press.

Good, T., and J. Brophy. 1997. *Contemporary educational psychology, 5th ed*. New York: Addison-Wesley.

Gross, J. L. Seeing is believing: Classroom demonstrations as scientific Inquiry. Retreived online July 2003 from *www.phy.ilstu.edu/ptefiles/312content/demos_as_inquiry*.

Hake, R. Lessons from the physics education reform effort. *Conservation Ecology* 5 (2): 28. retrieved online July 2003 from *www.consecol.org/vol5/iss2/art28*.

Hayes, M., and D. Deyhle. 2001. Connecting differences: A comparative study of curriculum differentiation. *The Science Teacher*, 85 (3), pp. 239–265.

Kujawa, S., and L. Huske. 1995. *The strategic teaching and reading project guidebook, rev. ed*. Oak Brook, IL: North Central Regional Educational Laboratory.

McDermott, L. C., and E. F. Redish. 1999. Resource letter: Physics education research. American *Journal of Physics*, 67, 755–767.

National Research Council (NRC). 2000. *Inquiry and the National Science Education Standards*. Washington, DC: National Academy Press.

National Research Council. 1996. *National Science Education Standards*. Washington, DC: National Academy Press.

Parkins, E. J. 1990. *Equilibrium, mind, and brain: Towards an integrated psychology.* New York: Prager.

Piaget, J. 1971. *Understanding causality.* New York: Norton.

Tifeten, B. *Creating learning environments to foster better attitudes.* Retrieved online July 2003, site no longer available.

Tulving, E. 1983. *Elements of episodic memory.* New York: Oxford University Press.

Willis, S. 1995. Reinventing science education: Reformers promote hands-on inquiry based learning. *Curriculum Update* Summer.

Wolff-M. R., C. J. McRobbie, K. B. Lucas, and S. Boutonne. 1997. Why may students fail to learn from demonstrations? A social practice perspective on learning in physics. *Journal of Research in Science Teaching* 34 (5): 509–533.